YANG STYLE
TAIJIQUAN

T'ai-Chi ch'üan

Morning Glory Publishers

Beijing, 1996

Editor: Yu Shenquan
Editorial consultants: Yang Yashan and Wang Junji
Photographer: Zhang Chunben
Cover illustration: Li Shiji

First edition 1988
Second edition 1991
Third edition 1996

Published by
Morning Glory Publishers
35 Chegongzhuang Xilu, Beijing 100044, China
Distributed by
China International Book Trading Corporation
35 Chegongzhuang Xilu, Beijing 100044, China
P.O.Box 399, Beijing, China
ISBN 7 - 5054 - 0481 - 4 /G·0100
02960
7 - E - 1682P
Printed in the People's Republic of China

CONTENTS

CONTENTS

FOREWORD

Yang Zhenduo

China is a nation with a long history and a splendid culture. The Chinese people have made great contributions to the civilization of the world, one of which is *taijiquan* which has become popular among the people of many countries and regions.

After the founding of new China in 1949, fruitful efforts have been made to inherit and carry forward *wushu,* a gem of China's cultural heritage, and *taijiquan,* a component of *wushu,* has developed as never before. In 1956, a simplified set of *taijiquan* (in 24 forms), based on the most popular sequences of the Yang Chengfu school, was compiled and popularized. This was followed three years later by the compilation of a more comprehensive set of *taijiquan* in 88 forms (referred to hereafter as "National Forms"). With the popularization of these National Forms, interest in the study and mastery of *taijiquan* of the Yang school soon spread across the nation.

While these developments gladden my heart in no small measure, I feel somewhat uneasy because there are not enough coaches for the growing number of *taijiquan* followers. As I had the opportunity to learn *taijiquan* from my father Yang Chengfu and elder brothers Yang Zhenming and Yang Zhenji in my youth, I would like to write down what I have learnt and record my experience which, I hope, will be of some value to all *taijiquan* enthusiasts.

Evolved from the Chen school of *taijiquan,* the Yang school has an unique style of its own. Its main characteristics are: a closely knit series of relaxed and composed, even and flowing movements that combine strength with resilience and vigour with gentleness, with the trunk erect as the axis of all movements.

Regular practice of this set of *tai*jiquan exercises will not only benefit one's physical well-being, but also give the trainee artistic enjoyment. It is extremely important, however, to perform correctly so as to bring out fully the unique style of the Yang school's *taijiquan.* I sincerely hope that this book will be of help to one and all.

Taijiquan has undergone 19 generations of development, from the last years of the Ming Dynasty (1368-1644) down to the present. Study and research of the methods and theories of this art have been carried out over the years by masters of the older generations, and the fruits of their work have provided us with important information for today's further exploration. It is no exaggeration to say that *taijiquan* would not have gained popularity today had it not been for the valuable work of past masters of the art. We must realize, however, that to make a direct reprint of the works of the past and present them to our students of today is not the best way. For one thing, those works were written mainly for people who had a good command of the fundamentals, and so the explanations of the methods of practice and ways of using the movements were too brief for beginners to follow.

In view of this, I have tried my best to make the explanations simple and easy to understand. The contents of this book consists of two parts:

1. General knowledge of the Yang school of *taijiquan*. This part includes *Talks on the Practice of Taijiquan* and *The Ten Essentials of Taijiquan*, which he narrated to his disciples, as well as illustrations of the traditional movements of the Yang school of *taijiquan*. There is also a chapter on how to comprehend and master the essentials of *taijiquan* based on my own experience, and answers to questions often confronting beginners. To help learners correct their mistakes, photos with explanations of wrong and right postures are attached.

2. Methods of practice and ways of using *taijiquan* movements constitute the main contents of the book. In the chapter on methods of practice, there are 104 photos of my father, 94 showing him doing the *taijiquan* movements and 10 doing the hand push, which were originally published in *A General Guide for Practice and Usage*. But as these photos only show the finishing posture of each form without the transitional movements, they may be difficult for beginners to follow. To overcome this drawback, a set of photos showing the transitional movements are added. It would be better if dotted and solid lines were drawn to depict each movement of the routine, but then this would have spoiled the genuineness of the photos. So I have refrained from doing so. As a compensation, more photos of the transitional movements, altogether 570, are given in this book.

The main contents of the chapter on the ways of using *taijiquan* movements are based on the book *Usage and Variations of Taijiquan, with Illustrated Demonstrations by Two*, written by my brother Yang Zhenming. In his book, there were 37 photos of my father doing *taijiquan*, which I intended to include in this chapter for our readers to imitate. But unfortunately the negatives have become too blurred and are not fit for reprinting. To make up

2

for this, I did my best to imitate his movements and had photos taken, but I doubt whether I have succeeded.

The ways of using *taijiquan* movements here are, of course, based on suppositions, and are designed according to the essentials of *taijiquan*. It is impossible to follow this pattern of movements when actually using them, for in an actual fight, for instance, the situations are much more complicated and they change rapidly. That is to say, one has to act on the spur of the moment and take steps suited to the circumstances. It is the mastery of the basic techniques that determine the ability to make the best use of the movements. Hence the importance of daily strict training according to the requirements in order to be able to use them to suit the occasion. No matter how one use them, one has to follow the basic rules. This is what is meant by "understand the rules, follow the rules and use them to the greatest advantage." It should be pointed out that the main purpose of the chapter on usage is to deepen the understanding of the trainees so that they can get the most benefit from it. Explanations on usage are therefore brief so that the trainees will learn the essence of the movements without following them mechanically.

Over the past three centuries, the popularity of *taijiquan* has increased and spread far beyond China's borders to Southeast Asia, Japan, Europe and America. This is an indication of its immense value to men's health, as has been testified by practice and research. *Taijiquan* is indeed a good exercise which, performed regularly, helps one keep fit, prevents and cures diseases, slows down the pace of growing old and prolongs life. This is perhaps why so many people, both at home and abroad, take to *taijiquan*, with some devoting to the research of its theory. It is my hope that this book will be of help to readers and will stimulate general interest in this traditional Chinese art. Any suggestions or comments on this book are sincerely welcome.

Here I would like to express my heartfelt thanks to Xie Wende, Li Jiren and others of the Institute of *Taijiquan* of the Yang School in Shanxi Province for the unstinting help they have given me in compiling this book.

3

THE EVOLUTION OF THE
YANG SCHOOL OF *TAIJIQUAN*

by Gu Liuxin

Yang Fukui (1799-1872), better knowa as Yang Luchan, was born in Yongnian County in north China's Hebei Province. Because of poverty, he had to leave his home village at the age of ten for Chenjiagou in Wenxian County in central China's Henan Province to make a living. He served as an attendant in the Chen family there and learned the "Lao Jia" ("Old Frame") style of *taijiquan* as well as "Tui Shou" (push-hands) and combat with weapons from the famous Chinese boxing master Chen Changxing (1771-1853). After thirty years of industrious study and practice, he returned to Yongnian. Before his departure for his home village, Chen Changxing told him that since he had become skilful *wushu* master, he would not have to worry about food and clothing for the rest of his life.

When Yang Luchan returned to Yongnian County, he put up at the Tai He Tang drugstore, which was run by the Chen family of Chenjiagou. The house belonged to the Wus, and their three brothers — Wu Chengqing, Wu Heqing and Wu Ruqing —were all enthusiasts of the folk martial art. They admired Yang Luchan's superb skill and learnt *wushu* from him.

The local people in Yongnian County held Yang Luchan in high esteem and praised his *taijiquan* as "cotton boxing", "soft boxing" or "solvent boxing" for its wonderful effects in overcoming the strong and beating the adversary without injuring him and for its flexible attacking and defending tactics.

At that time, Wu Ruqing was a councillor in the Sichuan office of the judicial department of the imperial court. He recommended Yang Luchan to teach *taijiquan* in the ancient capital city of Peking where many nobles and kinsmen of the Qing Dynasty learnt *wushu* from him. The House of Prince Duan, one of the royal families in the capital, had employed a large number of boxing masters and wrestlers, and some of them were anxious to have a trial of strength with Yang Luchan, but he invariably declined their challenge politely. One day a famous boxing master of high prestige insisted on competing with him to see who was the stronger. The boxer suggested that they sit on two chairs and pit their right fists against each other. Yang Luchan had no choice but to agree. Shortly after the contest began, that boxing master started to sweat all over and his chair creaked as if it was going to fall apart. But Yang Luchan looked as composed and serene as ever. Then he got up and in a gentle tone to the onlookers: "The master's skill is indeed superb. Only his chair is not as firmly made as mine." The man was so moved by his modesty that he never failed to praise Yang's exemplary conduct and unmatched *wushu* skill. Later on, whenever anyone wanted to try his prowess with Yang Luchan, he would throw the challenger to the ground without injuring him. In this way, Yang Luchan gained great fame and high prestige and was nicknamed "Yang the Invincible." He was later appointed a *wushu* officer in the Qing court with the rank higher than the seventh-grade official. When he paid a visit to Chenjiagou to see his old friends, he received a warm welcome.

At that time there was a *wushu* master named Liu who had taught thousands of students. One day he challenged Yang Banhou (1837-1892), who was one of Yang Luchan's sons, to a contest. Yang Banhou, who was then in the prime of youth and a bit bellicose by nature, accepted the challenge without hesitation. During the contest which attracted hundreds of people, Yang Banhou sent his opponent reeling to the ground several metres away with a stunning blow of his palm. Since then, Yang Banhou was also called "Yang the Invincible".

The number of people wishing to learn *wushu* began to increase. To meet popular needs, Yang Luchan gradually deleted from the series of movements such difficult actions as jumps and leaps, explosion of strength and vigorous foot stamping. After revisions by his third son Yang Jianhou (1839-1917), this series of movements came to be known as "*Zhong Jia*" (Medium Frame"). Later, it was again revised by Yang Chengfu (1883-1936), the third son of Yang Jianhou, which finally developed into the present "*Da Jia*" ("Big Frame") style because of its extended and natural posture, slow and even movements. It was different from his uncle Yang Banhou's style which was known under the name "*Xiao Jia*" ("Small Frame"). This is now the most popular Yang school of *taijiquan*.

The Yang school of *taijiquan* was born out of the Chen school of *taijiquan* which was known as "Lao Jia" ("Old Frame"). The movements are relaxed, even and graceful like the drifting clouds and flowing stream, quite unlike the Chen style which alternates slow with quick movements, and vigorous with restrained and controlled actions. The performance of the Yang style of *taijiquan* is terse and simple and always follows a circular path, just like "reeling off raw silk from a cocoon." The movements are naturally combined with breathing which should be deep and should "sink to the *dan tian*" (a point in the lower belly slightly below the navel). Here again it is quite different from the Chen style which combines "sink deep breath to the *dan tian*" with "breath circulation in the lower belly".

Good for the health and known for its curative effects, the Yang school of *taijiquan* which is easy to learn has caught the fancy of an increasing number of people, and that is why it is more popular than the Chen school.

The magnificent skill of three generations of the Yang family won them great renown throughout the capital. What was noteworthy was the fact that they unstintingly passed on their skill to many young people, which is perhaps one of the reasons why there are so many followers of the Yang school of *taijiquan* today. In 1928, Yang Chengfu was invited to teach *taijiquan* successively in Nanjing, Shanghai, Hangzhou, Guangzhou and Hankou. Thus the Yang school of *taijiquan* spread throughout the country.

Noted for its extended and natural postures, well-knit gentle and steady movements, the Yang style of *taijiquan* combines vigour with gentleness, with its actions following a circular path. Each and every form or movement contains the technique of countering and overpowering the adversary.

The Yang school of *taijiquan* has three "frame" forms — high, medium and low. The learner may determine the amount of exercise in accordance with his or her age, physical conditions and specific requirements (such as keeping fit, preventing and curing diseases, physical training and recreation and competition).

Because the movements are extended and natural, gentle and lissom, graceful and unique in style, as well as simple and easy to learn, the Yang school of *taijiquan* has won the favour of large number of *wushu* enthusiasts.

Yang Chengfu, one of the founders of this school, was a great *wushu* master of his time. Whenever he practised *taijiquan*, he strictly followed the routines and was never lax in his movements. This is evident from the illustrations in this book. The movements of his entire body embody the quintessence of *taijiquan* exercises. Yang Chengfu once said: *"Taijiquan* is an art with strength concealed in the gentle movements, like an 'iron hand in a velvet glove' or a needle concealed in cotton." He cautioned learners to always keep to the roundness and relaxation in their movements which, he said, must be gentle, natural, flexible and smooth as well as synchronized with one's mind. Actually, this is a summing-up of his own experience and attainment.

After Yang Chengfu came to the southern part of the country, he gradually realized that *taijiquan* had the efficacy of treating chronic disease, building up one's health and bringing longevity. When he gave *taijiquan* exhibitions in the "Zhirou *Wushu* Association" during his early days in Shanghai, which was set up by his disciple Chen Weiming, an editor working in the "Qing Dynasty History Institute", he performed the movements of kicking with speed and force. Later, however, to suit the needs of treating chronic disease, he changed them into slow movements with the inner exertion of force. And in such movements as punching downward and punching the opponent's pubic region, he only made imitations instead of manifest exertions of force, thus making the set of movements continuous and evenly-paced.

Yang Chengfu was a stalwart and handsome man. Creating a style all his own, he had mastered extraordinary skill in "Tui Shou" (push-hands) and was good at both attack and defence. Though his punches were delivered in a gentle manner, they were as hard as a steel bar wrapped in soft cloth. He could deliver a stunning blow with only little action, and no sooner had the opponent felt that he was attacked than he was flung several metres away without being hurt. While other schools might regard injuring the opponent as the main objective, Yang Chengfu merely overpowered the opponent without hurting him, thereby blazing a new trail for the art of attack in the martial arts. Small wonder many learners not only wanted to master the skill but enjoyed doing so.

Yang Shaohou (1862-1930), Yang Chengfu's elder brother, was also a famous *wushu* master who learnt most of his skills from his uncle Yang Banhou and, like his uncle, he was bellicose by nature. His *taijiquan* "frame" style was originally similar to his brother's, but later it gradually changed to the style of high "frame" with lively footwork and well-knit small movements, alternating quick with slow actions. He was swift and powerful in delivering his blows and, with eyes blazing like torches, a grim smile on his face and roaring and howling as he darted back and forth, he was held in awe by others. The technical features of this kind of *taijiquan* were: overcoming strong attacks with soft movements, adapting oneself to others' movements and following up with quick attacks, using the motion of "sudden connection" to defeat the opponent with surprise attacks. The hand movements included catching, pushing and capturing, injuring the attacker's muscles and harming his bones, attacking the opponent's vital points and "controlling" his arteries and veins, using "continuous" and "sudden connection" force to throw the attacker to the ground with lightning speed.

When teaching his pupils, Yang Shaohou would attack them without pulling his punches. His attacking movements were swift and ferocious, and his facial expression was changeable and varied. All this made it difficult for his trainees to imitate, which was why many of them dropped out halfway. And that was also perhaps why Yang Shaohou's style of *taijiquan* was not as popular as Yang Changfu's, though the two brothers enjoyed an equally high reputation during their lifetime.

Yang Shaohou followed his brother to the southern parts of the country and gave lectures in Shanghai and Nanjing. Mang officials and rich merchants vied with one another to learn from him.

Wu Jianquan, a famous master of the Wu style of *taijiquan*, invited Yang Shaohou to teach his son Wu Gongyi. After several months' coaching by Yang Shaohou, Wu Gongyi mastered the skills of catching, throwing and other techniques, which made him a better *wushu* expert than other disciples of the Wu school of *taijiquan*.

Yang Chengfu's techniques improved and matured with the passage of time. In his middle age, his *wushu* skill reached its apex, and his performance had that touch of magnificence and gallantry as few maestros could acquire. In the book *Taijiquan Techniques* written by his disciple Chen Weiming in 1925, there were 37 photographs showing Yang Chengfu in different postures and 4 photographs showing Yang Chengfu doing *"Tui Shou"* (push-hands) exercises with Xu Yusheng. In the book *A Manual of Taijiquan* compiled by Zheng Manqian in 1934 for Yang Chengfu, there were 104 photographs. Although Yang's weight was 290 pounds at that time, his movements were natural and relaxed, combining vigour with gentleness. It could be said that he had attained the acme of technical proficiency.

Among his students who later became great *taijiquan* masters and teachers were: Cui Yishi (Beijing), Li Chunnian (Sichuan Province), Chen Weiming, Wu Huichuan, Fu Zhongwen (Shanghai), Niu Chunming (Hangzhou), Dong Yingjie (Hongkong). Only Fu Zhongwei is still living today.

Yang Chengfu's eldest son, Yang Zhenming, has been teaching *taijiquan* in Hongkong for a long time. Yang Zhenji, his second son, is at present the chairman of the *wushu* association of the city of Handan in Hebei Province. Yang Zhenduo, the third son, is now teaching *taijiquan* in the city of Taiyuan in Shanxi Province and is also the chairman of the Research Association of the Yang school of *taijiquan* in that province. In November 1961 he went to Shanghai to give a *taijiquan* exhibition which caused a great sensation. Many *taijiquan* fans made a special trip to Shanghai to watch his performance.

Yang Chengfu had been to Shanghai on several occasions to teach *tai-jiquan,* and each time he took with him an assistant to do the "push-hand" duet. As I remember, the man who first accompanied him to Shanghai was Wu Huichuan (250 pounds in weight and a former wrestler); the second time he was accompanied by Dong Yingjie; the third time it was Yang Kairu; the fourth time, it was Chang Qingling; and the last time, it was Fu Zhongwen who was the son of Yang Chengfu's daughter.

The three generations of the Yang family had taught *taijiquan* for many years and had accumulated rich experience in this regard. With their teaching materials and methods constantly improved, the Yang school of *taijiquan* is now extremely popular among the Chinese people.

I have taken a fancy to *wushu* since childhood. In 1927 I joined the "Zhirou *Wushu* Association" in Shanghai and learnt *taijiquan* from Chen Weiming. I also learnt from Wu Huichuan and when Yang Chengfu and Yang Shaohou came to Shanghai, I had the privilege of benefiting from their personal instructions. From then on, I became more convinced than ever of the benefits of *taijiquan.*

I am now over 70 and I must say I owe my good health first to the improvement of living conditions after liberation and, second, to doing *taijiquan* and "push-hands" exercises.

In 1963 when I assisted Fu Zhongwen in compiling the book *The Yang School of Taijiquan,* I insisted that the illustrations should strictly conform to the postures in the photographs of Yang Chengfu so as to bring out the true characteristics of the Yang style of *taijiquan.*

I was pleased to learn that Yang Zhenduo had written a book to popularize the Yang school of *taijiquan,* and it gives me great pleasure to write a preface for it. I hereby offer a few commonplace remarks by way of introduction in the hope that it will help readers get some idea of the past and present of this school of *taijiquan.*

TALKS ON THE PRACTICE
OF *TAIJIQUAN*

Narrated by Yang Chengfu
Recorded by Zhang Hongkui

There are many schools of Chinese *wushu* (martial arts), all with technical skills based on philosophy. Since ancient times, many people have devoted their lifetime and energy to probing the nature and essence of *wushu* and mastering the maximum skills, but few have succeeded. However, a learner can improve his skill if he keeps on practising and someday he will become an expert. As the saying goes: Drops falling, if they fall constantly, will bore through a stone.

Taijiquan is part of the rich cultural heritage of China. It is an art in whose slow and gentle movements are embodied vigour and force. As a Chinese saying aptly puts it, "Inside the cotton is hidden a needle." Its technical, physiological and mechanical qualities all have a philosophical basis. For learners, the guidance of a good teacher and discussions of the skills and techniques with friends are necessary, but the most important thing is persistent and untiring practice. Indeed, there is nothing like practice, and learners of *taijiquan*, men and women, young and old, will get the best possible results if they keep at it all the year round.

In recent years, the number of people studying *taijiquan* in various parts of China has been increasing. This is an indication of the bright prospects of *wushu*. Many learners are conscientious and persistent in training, which will enable them to attain a high level of achievement. It should be pointed out here that two wrong tendencies should be guarded against. The first is that some people who are young and talented acquired a quicker understanding than most other people and so become complacent and stop halfway. These people can never achieve great success. The second wrong tendency is that some learners are too anxious to achieve quick success and get instant benefits. They want to learn everything in a short time, from shadow boxing to wielding the sword, broadsword, spear and other weapons. They know a smattering of each, but do not grasp the essence and their movements and postures are full of flaws to the expert eye. It is difficult to correct their movements, for a thorough "overhaul" is needed and, as often as not, they might change in the morning and return to the old habits in the evening. Hence the saying in Chinese boxing circles: "Learning *taijiquan* is easy but to correct a wrong style is difficult." In other words, more haste, less speed. And if these people pass on their mistakes to others, they will be doing a great harm.

In learning *taijiquan*, one should first of all start from the *quan jia* or frame of boxing; he should practise according to the routines and follow the master's every movement carefully, and keep each action in mind. Meanwhile, he should pay attention to *nei, wai, shang* and *xia. Nei* means using the mind rather than force. *Wai* means the relaxation of the limbs, shoulders and elbows, making the movements from the foot and leg to the waist gentle and continuous. *Shang* means straightening the head, and *xia* means sinking the breath to the lower belly.

For a beginner, the most important thing is to remember these points, grasp their essence and practise each basic movement correctly over and over again, never seeking quick success and instant benefit. It is advisable to make slow and steady progress, for this will pay in the long run. In practising *taijiquan,* it is necessary to keep all the joints of the body relaxed, so that the movements will be natural and unrestrained. Do not hold your breath (that may lead to puff and blow), and do not use stiff strength in moving the arms, legs, waist and body, but try to make your movements gentle and continuous. These two points are well-known among the *wushu* experts, but many trainees have difficulty in putting them into practice.

The learners should bear in mind the following points:

(1) Keep your head erect and do not incline it forward or backward. As a saying goes, "It's like there is something on your head, and you should take care not to let it fall." But you should not hold your head in a stiff manner, and though your eyes look straight ahead, they should follow the movements of the limbs and body. Although your eyes look into vacancy, they are an important component of the movements of the body as a whole. Your mouth should remain half open and half closed, with the nose breathing in and the mouth breathing out naturally. If saliva is produced in the mouth swallow it.

(2) Hold the torso straight and the backbone and free end of the sacrum vertical. When moving, always keep the chest slightly inward and back upright. The beginners should keep these key points in mind, otherwise their movements will become a mere formality or dull-looking, and they will not be able to make much progress in spite of long years of practice.

(3) Relax the joints of both arms, letting the shoulders droop and the elbows curve naturally; the palms should be slightly extended and the fingers slightly bent. Move the arms by consciousness and send *qi* (breath or vital energy) to the fingers. Remember these key points and success will be yours.

(4) Take note of the difference in stance between the two legs which move as gently as these of a cat. When one foot is planted firmly on the ground, the other is in an empty stance. When you shift the weight on to the left leg, then the left foot is firmly on the ground, while the right foot is in an empty stance, and vice versa. Though the foot is in an empty stance it is always ready to move. When the foot is firmly on the ground, it does not mean you should exert too much force with that leg, for if you do so, your body will incline forward and you will lose your balance.

(5) The action of the feet is divided into kicking upward and kicking downward. When you kick upward, pay attention to your toes, and when you kick downward, pay attention to the sole; consciousness of the action will be followed by vital energy, and vital energy will be followed by strength. When you do all this, you should relax the joints and avoid stiffness.

In practising *taijiquan,* one should first master and practise the "frame" as above mentioned (bare-handed forms), such as *taiji* shadow boxing and *changquan* (long shadow boxing); then one can proceed to single-hand pushing, one-site pushing, pushing with feet moving and free-hand fighting, and after a period one can take exercises with weapons such as *taiji* sword, *taiji* scimitar and *taiji* spear.

Learners should practise regularly every morning or before going to bed. It is preferable to practise seven or eight times during the daytime; if one is hard pressed for time, then practise at least once in the morning and once in the evening. Do not practise immediately after meals or after drinking. The best place is in the gardens or parks where the air is fresh and the environment conducive to health. Do not practise on windy days or in a filthy place. for when you do the exercise, you might breathe in too much dust or dirt which is harmful to your lungs. It is advisable to put on sportswear and comfortable cloth or rubber shoes. When you sweat, don't take off your clothes or wipe with cold towels, lest you should catch cold and fall ill.

THE TEN ESSENTIALS
OF *TAIJIQUAN*

Narrated by Yang Chengfu
Recorded by Chen Weiming

(1) Straightening the Head

Stand straight and hold the head and neck naturally erect, with the mind concentrated on the top. Do not strain or be tense; otherwise, the blood and vital energy cannot circulate smoothly.

(2) Correct Position of Chest and Back

keep chest slightly inward, which will enable you to sink your breath to the *dan tian* (lower belly). Do not protrude your chest, otherwise you will feel uneasy in breathing and somewhat "top heavy".

Great force can be launched from the spine only when you keep the vital energy in your lower belly.

(3) Relaxation of Waist

For the human body, the waist is the dominant part. When you relax the waist, your two feet will be strong enough to form a firm base. All the movements depend on the action of the waist, as the saying goes: "Vital force comes from the waist." Inaccurate movements in *taijiquan* stem from the erroneous actions of the waist.

(4) Solid and Empty Stance

It is of primary importance in *taijiquan* to distinguish between "Xu" (Empty) and "Shi" (Solid). If you shift the weight of the body on to the right leg, then the right leg is solidly planted on the ground and the left leg is in an empty stance. When your weight is on the left leg, then the left leg is firmly planted on the ground and the right leg is in an empty stance. Only in this way can you turn and move your body adroitly and without effort, otherwise you will be slow and clumsy in your movements and not able to remain stable and firm on your feet.

(5) Sinking of Shoulders and Elbows

Keep your shoulder in natural, relaxed position. If you lift your shoulders, the *qi* will rise with them, and the whole body will be without strength. You should also keep the elbows down, otherwise you will not be able to keep your shoulders relaxed and move your body with ease. ·

(6) Using the Mind Instead of Force

Among people who practise *taijiquan,* it is quite common to hear this comment: "That is entirely using the mind, not force." In practising *taijiquan,* the whole body is relaxed, and there is not an iota of stiff or clumsy strength in the veins or joints to hinder the movement of the body. People may ask: How can one increase his strength without exercising force? According to traditional Chinese medicine, there is in the human body a system of pathways called *jingluo* (or meridian) which link the viscera with different parts of the body, making the human body an integrated whole. If the *jingluo* is not impeded, then the vital energy will circulate in the body unobstructed. But if the *jingluo* is filled with stiff strength, the vital energy will not be able to circulate and consequently the body cannot move with ease. One should therefore use the mind instead of force, so that vital energy will follow in the wake of the mind or consciousness and circulate all over the body. Through persistent practice one will be able to have genuine internal force. This is what *taijiquan* experts call "Lithe in appearance, but powerful in essence."

A master of *taijiquan* has arms which are as strong as steel rods wrapped in cotton, with immense power concealed therein. Boxers of the "Outer School" (a branch of *wushu* with emphasis on attack, as opposed to the "Inner School" which places the emphasis on defence) look powerful when they exert force, but when they cease to do so, the power no longer exists. So it is merely a kind of superficial force.

(7) Coordination of Upper and Lower Parts

According to the theory of *taijiquan,* the root is in the feet, the force is launched through the legs, controlled by the waist, and expressed by the fingers; the feet, the legs and the waist form a harmonious whole. When the hands, the waist and the legs move, the eyes should follow their movements. This is meant by coordination of the upper and lower parts. If any one part should cease to move, then the movements will be disconnected and fall into disarray.

(8) Harmony Between the Internal and External Parts

In practising *taijiquan,* the focus is on the mind and consciousness. Hence the saying: "The mind is the commander, and the body is subservient to it." With the tranquillity of the mind, the movements will be gentle and graceful. As far as the "frame" is concerned, there are only the *Xu* (empty), *shi* (solid), *kai* (open) and *he* (close). *Kai* not only means opening the four limbs but the mind as well, and *he* means closing the mind along with the four limbs. Perfection is achieved when one unifies the two and harmonizes the internal and external parts into a complete whole.

(9) Importance of Continuity

In the case of the "Outer School" (which emphasizes attack) of boxing, the strength one exerts is stiff and the movements are not continuous, but are sometimes made off and on, which leave openings the opponent may take advantage of. In *taijiquan,* one focuses the attention on the mind instead of force, and the movements from beginning to end are continuous and in an endless circle, just "like a river which flows on and on without end" or "like reeling the silk thread off cocoons."

(10) Tranquillity in Movement

In the case of the "Outer School" of boxing, the emphasis is on leaping, bouncing, punching and the exertion of force, and so one often gasps for breath after practising. But in *taijiqu*an, the movement is blended with tranquillity, and while performing the movements, one maintains tranquillity of mind. In practising the "frame," the slower the movement, the better the results. This is because when the movements are slow, one can take deep breath and sink it to the *dan tian.* It has a soothing effect on the body and mind.

Learners of *taijiquan* will get a better understanding of all this through careful study and persistent practice.

SOME IMPORTANT POINTS
CONCERNING THE YANG SCHOOL
OF *TAIJIQUAN*

Yang Zhenduo

I. Relaxation

It is easy to understand the literal meaning of "relaxation". The word here has two implications: (1) The relaxation of the mind, that is, the elimination of all other thoughts and the concentration of the mind on practising *taijiquan* (2) The relaxation of the whole body and the elimination of the stiff strength inside it. The second implication has indeed caused some misunderstanding among many learners. They take it for granted that relaxation means not using any strength and that they should display physical softness. The fact that the "Ten Essentials of *Taijiquan*" emphasizes the employment of the mind instead of the use of strength gives rise to another misunderstanding that *taijiquan* should be all softness. Some people, of course, have doubts on this point, since there is the saying that "the needle is hidden in the cotton" or "vigour is concealed in gentleness." Where exactly does vigour lie? Some people have probed into this question with experiments and they have discovered that the conscious employment of even a little strength results in a stiff feeling, while relaxation indeed brings a feeling of softness. It is therefore natural that the beginner finds himself in a dilemma.

II. What is Real Relaxation?

I would like to give some of my personal views on this question. Though relaxation means the conscious relaxation of the mind, more importantly, it means the relaxation of the whole body.

Relaxation of the whole body means the conscious relaxation of all the joints, and this organically links up all parts of the body in a better way. This does not mean softness. It requires a lot of practice in order to understand this point thoroughly. Relaxation also means the "stretching" of the limbs, which gives you a feeling of heaviness. (This feeling of heaviness or stiffness is a concrete reflection of strength.) This feeling is neither a feeling of softness nor of stiffness, but somewhere in between. It should not be confined to a specific part, but involves the whole body. It is like molten iron under high temperature. So relaxation "dissolves" stiff strength in very much the same way. Stiff strength, also called "clumsy strength", undergoes a qualitative change after thousands of times of "dissolution" exercises. Just like iron which can be turned steel, so "clumsy strength" can be turned into force, and relaxation is a means of gradually converting it into force. Our ancestors put it well: "Conscious relaxation will unconsciously produce force." There is truth in this statement.

III. The Difference Between Strength and Force

Strength can be compared to unheated and unmelted pig iron. It is inborn and is distributed over all parts of the body. When a baby is born, it cries and moves its limbs with its natural strength. When we say we should not use strength in *taijiquan,* we refer to this natural strength (clumsy strength). We should instead use force, which is also called "internal force", or *taijiquan* force, Though force is not natural strength, it is difficult to separate the two. In other words, despite their difference, there is no clear-cut demarcation line between them. Force derives from strength, which serves as its basis. Iron becomes steel through heating and tempering, so steel derives from iron. If we do not have a proper understanding of this fact, we will counterpose one against the other and fail to have a correct understanding of the relationship between the two. Consequently, we will not be able to achieve what has been described as "The needle is hidden in the cotton" or "vigour is concealed in gentleness." Gentleness here suggests a degree of tenacity. Only when we have acquired such an understanding can we achieve what is summarized as "Relaxation gives rise to gentleness, which in turn gives rise to vigour, and gentleness and vigour supplement each other."

IV. How Should We Understand "Employment of the Mind Instead of the Use of Strength".

This is easy to understand when we know the difference between strength and force.

Now let us return to the topic of strength which, as has been said, is inborn and is distributed over all parts of the body. When we start doing exercises every day, we should first of all 'relax' in the conscious search of strength. Then, we gather the strength, organize it under our command before we put it into exercise. Gradually the scattered strength becomes a totality in itself. This is like a well-trained army which moves in unison according to the order issued by its commander. In this way, the army can achieve its goal. Our forerunners said: "Whither the mind goes, force follows." That is to say, when the learner has attained a certain level after persistent training and is able to combine force with skill, then force will emerge of itself and follow the mind. This is a point I wish to drive home.

A strong man who has never learnt *wushu* may be able to defeat his opponent. This of course depends on who his opponent is. However, given the same physical conditions, a *wushu* expert is sure to defeat an opponent who has not practised *wushu*. A man of strong build will of course become stronger if he takes up *wushu* and persists in training.

TAIJIQUAN—AN EXERCISE FOR THE WHOLE BODY

Yang Zhenduo

Taijiquan is an exercise for the whole body, and it trains both the mind and the body. The waist is of primary importance, for it leads the movement of the four limbs. In practising *taijiquan*, when one part moves, all the other parts also move, with the upper and lower limbs following accordingly. All this points to the totality of its movements. However, many learners often tend to divide the body into three parts consciously or unconsciously: the arms, the trunk and the legs. The result is that each part moves on its own, without any connection whatsoever with the other parts. While the legs and the arms move independently, the movements of the trunk, including the buttocks, the back, the abdomen and the internal organs, are neglected. If this should happen, the desired effects cannot be achieved. In this regard, I would like to stress a few points which I hope learners will keep in mind.

(1) Because of its position, the waist performs the special function of linking up all parts of the body — the hips and the legs below and the back, the arms and the head above. So in doing the exercises, we must make sure that the waist, which is the central link, coordinates the movements of the upper part and the lower part of the body, and that we have a kind of feeling all over the body, which is actually the feeling of force at work. While all the parts coordinate, they interact on each other. Without the relaxation of the waist and the hips, it is not possible to keep the chest in a natural position and exercise the muscles on the back. Only in this way can the vital energy reach the back and force emit from the spine. It is impossible for the upper limbs to emit force without the relaxation of the waist and the hips, the coordination of the lower limbs and the exertion of force by the legs which serve as the base. That is why we must understand the essential points thoroughly and strive for the harmony of the movements. Our ancestors told us to "take the waist as the axis and use it to lead the movements of the four limbs." But we should here include the trunk, for when the main axis moves, all the other parts of the body will follow suit.

(2) One more point must be made clear. "The root or the base is in the feet." The meaning of "feet" here includes the legs. We must feel the force

of the straightening and kicking movements of the feet. The base will not be firm without the straightening or propping movements of the legs, and the result will not be difficult to imagine. How are we then to do the stepping, straightening or propping and kicking movements correctly? When you stretch out the leg on which you put your weight, the leg must be propped up in the shape of a bow; then you feel the force moving from this leg to the other leg on which you have not put your weight. You must not stretch out your leg without feeling the force, otherwise the movements of the whole body will fall into disarray. You will understand this after careful observation through practice. Failing to do so, it will be difficult to achieve the continuity and totality of *taijiquan* movements.

With regard to the coordination between the upper and lower limbs, especially coordination between the two arms, we must see to it that the waist brings along the back and the arms, which in turn bring along the wrists. We should also pay attention to the natural lowering of the shoulders and elbows, the poise of the wrist and the palms, the slight bending of the fingers and the right spacing between the fingers, which are all important in *taijiquan*.

CORRECT AND WRONG FORMS, POSTURES AND MOVEMENTS

Yang Zhenduo

Forms of Hands

Whether the form of the hands is pleasing to the eye or not means whether or not the movements of the hands will be smooth and comfortable. More important, it means whether or not your hands can give expression to the skill and strength of your whole body. Of course, our main purpose in doing *taijiquan* exercises today is to improve our health and cure diseases. In this respect, if both hands move in a smooth and comfortable way, they will play an important role in facilitating blood circulation and metabolism. Please look at the following forms of the hands:

Fig. 1

The hand in the above figure is formed by stretching the palm slightly, with the fingers slightly bent and a little apart. In this way, it looks evenly balanced and comfortable.

Fig. 1   Fig. 2   Fig. 3

The above figures show that the fingers are either closed, too far apart, too upright or bent too much. These forms are all incorrect.

The Connection Between Hand, Wrist and Arm

What do the following figures show? They show us the correct way of keeping the wrist erect and the fingers a little apart in practising *taijiquan*.

Fig. 1

The above figure shows that the hands, wrist and arm are well coordinated. This form shows in a perfect way the inner strength and connection between the hand, wrist and arm. They appear to be mild and gentle, but not loose and lifeless, nor stiff and rigid. This is the proper way of coordinating the movements of the hand, wrist and arm.

But the following two ways of holding the hand, wrist and arm are wrong. In the first case, they seem to be disconnected and appear limp and lifeless, as if the man is listless and in low spirits. In the other case, the wrist is stiff, that is, exerting stiff force with the wrist, which not only hampers movement but also hinders blood circulation, and therefore adversely affects training. Moreover, it gives an uncomfortable feeling. This is well illustrated in the following two figures.

Fig. 2   Fig. 3

How to Turn the Body with the Arms
Moving Horizontally

In performing the action of moving both arms in arcs in the "Single Whip", while moving outward, the left arm plays the leading role and the right arm follows it; the left hand is bent inward and the wrist is kept level. There should be a feeling of holding the shoulders and elbows down, sinking the wrist and keeping the fingers a bit apart; the hands and arms should be well coordinated and strength put into them. You must not move the arm in a stiff and listless manner. In moving back, the right arm plays the leading role and the left arm follows it; the wrist should be kept level and the hands and arms well coordinated. This is well illustrated below.

Fig. 1

The left wrist is kept level; the arm and hand are well coordinated, and strength is put into them.

Fig. 2

The two hands are stiff, with no difference between the primary and the secondary.

Fig. 3

It is wrong to incline forward or backward.

Various Forms of the Lower Limbs

To form the "Bow Step", you bend the front leg and straighten the rear one. The front foot points forward, while the rear foot is turned outward (45 degrees). The two feet are approximately shoulder-width apart, if the distance is too wide, your posture will be wrong and if it is too narrow, you will stand on the same line, which means you will not be able to maintain your balance. The form in Fig. 1 better suits the requirements. In Fig. 2 you stand on the same line, and in Fig. 3 the distance between the two feet is too wide.

Fig. 1   Fig. 2   Fig. 3

How to Bend the Knee in the "Bow Step"

When you bend your left leg to form the left "bow step", the knee and the toes of the left foot should be in a perpendicular line as in Fig. 1.

In Fig. 2 the knee goes beyond the toes of the foot, which means the weight will be shifted too far forward and you will not be able to remain firm on your feet.

In Fig. 3, the knee is behind the toes of the foot, which makes it impossible for your lower limbs to exert force.

Fig. 1   Fig. 2   Fig. 3

The following three illustrations show the action of standing on one leg. The leg on which you stand should be straight, not stiff or curved. Keep your leg straight, but not over-stretched. The form in Fig. 1 is correct.

Fig. 1   Fig. 2

In Fig. 2, the leg is bent, so you cannot put forth strength.

Fig. 3

In Fig. 3, the leg is stiff, and all the strength is put in the shank. In this way, you not only feel uncomfortable, but will incline your upper limbs forward, making it impossible for you to maintain proper balance.

The Correct Way of Performing the Movement of "Empty Step with Heel Coming Down on the Floor and Toes Raised".

Fig. 1

In the above illustration, the toes are slightly raised, which is the correct form. If the toes are turned upward in a stiff way, as in the following illustration, all the strength will be put in the ankle, and the result is your left leg will be stiff and will be disconnected with the other parts.

Fig. 2

In practising *taijiquan*, you should hold the shoulders and elbows down, which is one of the actions of keeping the whole body relaxed. Only in this

Fig. 1

way can you connect the back with the arms and coordinate the movements of the whole body. (See Fig. 1)

If you dangle your arms, you will feel suffocated because you cannot raise your breath. You will feel top heavy and the lower part of your body will not be able to remain stable. This is an important point to remember. See Fig. 2 and you will get the point.

Fig. 2

The following illustrations show what you must do and not do in order to keep the body erect and comfortable in practising *taijiquan*. You should not arch your back, bend your waist, stick up your hips or bend backward, otherwise your posture will not be comfortable or pleasing to the eye. In Fig. 1, the movement is smooth and comfortable and therefore correct.

Fig. 1

In the following illustrations, the postures give an uncomfortable feeling.

How should you clench your fist for the various punches? This is explained as follows.

1. "Deflect Downward, Parry and Punch": This is divided into two

Fig. 2

Fig. 3

Fig. 4

Fig. 5

kinds: bending the wrist downward while clenching the fist and turning the wrist over to clench the fist. They are used in "Deflect Downward" and you clench your right fist, close the fingers and keep the back of the fist level; but you should not clench the fist too tightly with stiff strength, neither should you clench a hollow fist. See the following ways of clenching the fist in "Deflect Downward, Parry and Punch".

Bend wrist downward and clench fist

Turn wrist over and clench fist

2. **"Chop Opponent with Fist":** In this form, the action is also to turn

the wrist over and clench the fist. But here you hit the opponent with the back of the fist. The following illustration shows how the fist is clenched.

Fig. 1

3. "Fist under Elbow": For this kind of punch, you should bend the fist inward and hit the opponent's chest with the face of the fist as shown in the following two illustrations.

Fig. 2

Fig. 3

The following two ways of clenching the fist, one hollow and the other stiff "dead" fist, are incorrect.

Hollow fist

Dead fist

4. "Strike Opponent's Ears with Both Fists": For this kind of punch, the fists are clenched in a way so that the parts between the thumb and the index finger obliquely face each other; you bend the arms and fists inward,

and hit the opponent's head with the parts between the thumb and the index finger close to the face of the fist and shown in the folowing illustration.

Fig. 1

The following illustration shows both arms straightened, with the parts between the thumb and the index finger directly facing each other and the fists hollow. This is not the correct way.

Fig. 2

Another kind of punch is in "Shoot the Tiger with Bow". Though both fists face outward, the parts between the thumb and the index finger obliquely face each other, one above the other. You should bend the left fist upward and the right fist downward. Try to get the hang of it.

Only a few examples are given above, with explanations and illustrations for the learners' reference. While you practise *taijiquan*, you should pay attention to many other movements and postures such as bending the head forward or backward, inclining the head to the one side and so on, which will not be dealt with here one by one. What is important is to grasp the main points and practise *taijiquan* conscientiously and strictly according to the routines. That is to say, you should follow the rules, for only in this way can you achieve the desired results in practising *taijiquan*.

NAMES OF THE FORMS OF THE YANG SCHOOL OF *TAIJIQUAN*

Yang Zhenduo

Form 1 Preparatory Form
Form 2 Commencing Form
Form 3 Grasp the Bird's Tail
Form 4 Single Whip
Form 5 Raise Hands and Step Up
Form 6 White Crane Spreads Its Wings
Form 7 Brush Knee and Twist Step (Left Style)
Form 8 Hand Strums the Lute
Form 9 Brush Knee and Twist Step (Left Style)
Form 10 Brush Knee and Twist Step (Right Style)
Form 11 Brush Knee and Twist Step (Left Style)
Form 12 Hand Strums the Lute
Form 13 Brush Knee and Twist Step (Left Style)
Form 14 Step Up, Deflect Downward, Parry and Punch
Form 15 Apparent Close-up
Form 16 Cross Hands
Form 17 Carry the Tiger to the Mountain
Form 18 Fist Under Elbow
Form 19 Step Back and Repulse the Monkey (Right Style)
Form 20 Step Back and Repulse the Monkey (Left Style)
Form 21 Step Back and Repulse the Monkey (Right Style)
Form 22 Slant Flying
Form 23 Raise Hands and Step Up
Form 24 White Crane Spreads Its Wings
Form 25 Brush Knee and Twist Step (Left Style)
Form 26 Needle at Sea Bottom
Form 27 Fan Through the Back
Form 28 Chop Opponent with Fist
Form 29 Step Up, Deflect Downward, Parry and Punch
Form 30 Step Up and Grasp the Bird's Tail
Form 31 Single Whip

ILLUSTRATIONS OF THE YANG SCHOOL OF *TAIJIQUAN*

Form 1   Preparatory Form

Stand naturally upright with feet shoulder-width apart, toes pointing forward, arms hanging naturally with palms facing inward and fingers pointing downward. Hold body erect, facing towards the south and looking straight forward. Keep the whole body relaxed. (Fig. 1).

Fig. 1

Points to remember:

(1) Be relaxed and natural but with the mind alert and concentrated; banish all thoughts so as to be in a tranquil state of mind.

(2) "Straighten the head as if there were something on it"; "Sink breath into abdomen"; "Loosen waist with sacrum right in the middle"; "Keep chest and back in their natural positions"; "Hold shoulders and elbows down".

(3) The above-mentioned points, which are the basis in practising *taijiquan*, should be followed throughout the process and kept in mind all the time. These basic points will not be repeated in the following forms.

Form 2   Commencing Form

(1) Turn arms slightly inward with palms pressed down a bit. Then move palms obliquely downward until they are placed beside the hips (Fig. 2)

Fig. 2

(2) Slowly raise arms forward and upward to shoulder level with palms turned from inside downward and fingers pointing forward, keeping the arms shoulder-width apart all the time.   (Fig. 3)

(3) With elbows slightly bent, move wrists downward slowly and place

Fig. 3

them beside the hips with palms facing downward and fingers pointing forward. ((Fig. 4)

Fig. 4

Points to remember:

(1) Be relaxed right from the beginning. This is not only means to dispel tense feelings but, more important, to consciously keep all the joints of the body loose, which will sort of stretch the joints to connect the parts between them into an organic whole. In this way, you will really feel relaxed.

(2) When raising the arms, avoid stiffness or rigidity and limpness or inertia in movement.

Form 3   Grasp the Bird's Tail

1. Ward Off Slantingly Upward (Left Style)

(1) When forearms are move downward and just before they reach bottom, shift weight slightly to the left and turn body to the right (45 degrees) with the force of the waist. At the same time, raise the sole of right foot slightly off the ground and then turn foot 45 degrees outward with heel on floor. Bend both forearms slightly inward with palms turned obliquely downward. (Fig. 5).

Fig. 5

(2) While bending right knee and squatting down towards the toes of right foot, shift weight on to right leg and bend left leg naturally and slightly into empty step without moving its position. At the same time, bend right forearm from below outward, upward and then inward until it is between chest and abdomen with the palm facing downward. Turn left forearm inward, then bend it inward until it is in front of abdomen with palm turned obliquely upward. (Fig. 6)

Fig. 6   Fig. 7

(3) After right leg is firm on the floor, move left leg forward with heel landing first on the floor and the sole slightly raised. (Fig. 7)

(4) As soon as left foot lands on the floor, shift weight to the left to form a left bow step. with right leg straightened. Meanwhile, push left forearm from below upward, raise hand and bend it slightly inward with palm turned obliquely inward. Move right forearm downward until it is in front of right hip, with palm facing downward. Look straight ahead with face turned due west. (Fig. 8)

II. Ward Off Slantingly Upward (Right Style)

(1) While shifting weight slightly to the rear, turn body to the right

(45 degrees) with the force of the waist. At the same time, turn left foot inward (45 degrees). (Fig. 9)

Fig. 8   Fig. 9

(2) While turning body from right to left (45 degrees) with the force of the waist, gradually shift weight on to left leg and change right leg into empty step with heel slightly off the ground. At the same time, move right forearm along with waist from right to left and bend it until it is below left forearm and in front of abdomen, with palm turned obliquely upward. Bend left forearm slightly inward to the left (45 degrees), with palm turned obliquely downward. (Fig. 10)

(3) When left leg is firm on the floor, raise right foot and take a step forward, with heel landing first on the floor and the sole slightly raised. (Fig. 11)

(4) With the support of the left leg, kick forward with right leg and then bend it to form a right bow step. At the same time, push right forearm upward from the left to the front until it is in front of the chest, with palm turned slightly inward; bend left forearm slightly inward until it is below the right forearm, with palm turned outward. Place left hand between the elbow and wrist of right forearm, with the fingertips about a fist away from right forearm and face turned due west. (Fig. 12)

Fig. 10   Fig. 11

Fig. 12

Points to remember:

Ward Off Slantingly Upward (Right and Left Styles)

(1) The turning of the body should follow the movement of the waist. They should not turn outward or inward by themselves.

(2) The turning of the right foot outward and the left foot inward should also follow the movement of the waist. They should not turn outward or inward by themselves.

(3) When bending leg forward to shift the weight, attention should be paid to coordinate the force of kicking and supporting so that the movement of the waist will carry along with it the movement of the four limbs. And when bending the leg, the knee should not go beyond the tiptoe.

(4) When the arms are pushed up, they should be at shoulder level. Hold the upper part of the body erect and draw hips in. Be sure where to put the weight of the body in each movement.

III. Pull Back

(1) When turning body from front to right (45 degrees) with the waist leading the movement, both forearms turn gradually along with hands until right palm obliquely outward and left palm faces obliquely inward; thus the palms face each other and the face is turned towards the northwest. (Fig. 13)

Fig. 13

(2) With the waist leading the movement, pull both arms back from the right, across the front, to the left (45 degrees). At the same time, shift weight gradually on to left leg and sit firmly on it. Change right leg into empty stance, with face turned towards the southwest. (Fig. 14)

Fig. 14

Points to remember:

(1) While the arms are being turned, the movement must follow that of the waist, and the change of palms must follow that of the arms. The movements of the palms and the forearms should be coordinated and must not be carried out independently.

(2) While arms are being moved, they should not be kept close to the body. The arms and armpits should be kept about a fist away from the body.

IV. Press Forward

(1) Following the inward turn of the right forearm, the right palm is also turned until it faces obliquely inward; following the outward turn of the left forearm, the left palm is also turned until it faces obliquely outward. Place left palm on right forearm near the wrist. (Fig. 15)

(2) With the front leg as support, straighten rear leg. Move weight gradually forward, bend right leg to form a right bow step. Following the movement of the waist, both arms press forward, with face turned due west.

42

(Fig. 16)

Fig. 15

Fig. 16

Points to remember:

(1) While pressing forward, do not raise your shoulders or protrude your hips, and the right arm should look as if it is going to push upward.

(2) The left palm must be kept close to the right forearm so as to help it exert its strength to the full.

(3) The left shoulder should be lowered slightly; do not let the tip of the elbow dangle.

V. Push

(1) With arms shoulder-width apart, move left arm forward and leftward, with palm facing obliquely downward; turn right arm inward, with palm turned downward. (Fig. 17)

Fig. 17   Fig. 18

(2) Straighten front leg backward, with rear leg leaning forward in support. With a movement of the waist, shift weight backward and gradually sit firmly on left leg. Bend elbows and draw hands backward to the front of chest, with wrists hanging slightly downward and palms facing forward. (Fig. 18)

(3) Push arms forward with the movement of the waist. At the same

time, bend right leg to form a right bow step, with face turned due west. (Fig. 19)

Fig. 19

Points to remember:

(1) While drawing arms in towards chest, see that the movement has the effect of holding the elbows down. Do not draw in softly or push out stiffly, nor draw in and push forward with stiff strength.

(2) In Figs. 18-19, when sitting on left leg, guard against leaning backward, and when moving forward to form a bow step, guard against leaning forward.

(3) When stretching arms forward, bend elbows slightly downward, instead of keeping them straight.

(4) After drawing in the hands to the front of the chest, lift them slightly and then move them downward in a small arc and push them forward. That is, do not push hands forward immediately after drawing them in.

Form 4   Single Whip

(1) Move arms slightly downward and turn palms from facing the front to facing downward. Then bend left arm slightly inward with palm facing

downward as if it is going to press down. Shift weight backward and sit on the left leg with the sole of right foot lifted slightly off the ground. (Fig. 20)

Fig. 20

(2) Following the movement of the waist, turn body and four limbs from right to left, with the right foot turned inward (135 degrees). At the same time, with the left arm taking the lead, move both arms in a large arc to the rear of the body (225 degrees). When left arm is straight and points towards the northeast, move right arm in a circle to the front of the chest with elbow and arm bent, then shift weight gradually on to right leg and sit firmly on it. (Figs. 21-22)

(3) Turn body, along with waist and arms, from left to right. Stretch right hand from inside outward to the southwest (45 degrees), and bend left forearm inward to front of chest. (Fig. 23)

(4) Hook right hand and turn left arm, with palm facing inward. (Fig. 24)

(5) Keeping arms still, first stretch left foot to the outside and front of right foot, with its heel landing first on the floor, and then following the movement of the waist, turn from the right to facing the front. Keeping right arm still, move left arm in a curve from right to left and from inside to outside and slowly stretch it out, with palm facing the front. At the same

Fig. 21

Fig. 22

Fig. 23

Fig. 24

time, bend left leg forward to form a left bow step, with face turned due east. (Fig. 25-26)

Fig. 25　　　　　　　　　　　　　Fig. 26

Points to remember:

(1) The movement of turning arms in an arc should follow that of the waist. At the same time, shifting of weight from left leg on to right one should also follow the waist. The left arm first takes the lead, with the right arm following it; then conversely, the right arm takes the lead, with the left arm following it. The action of arms must be well coordinated so that the movements will be round and smooth.

(2) Keep the upper part of body erect, with chest and back in their natural positions; loosen waist and hips, hold shoulders and elbows down all the time. Failing to do so, it is possible that, in the course of turning, there will be the protruding of hips, the bending of waist and other defects.

(3) Head should turn along with body. Eyes should follow the direction of the turning of the main hand, but should not remain fixed on the hand.

(4) In Fig. 26, both arms should be kept horizontal, and the rear arm should not be too high.

(5) To form hooked hand, bend wrist downward, and bunch the five erect fingers. Fingers should not be bent and fingertips should not be bunched too tightly. In Fig. 26, the direction of the right arm with the hooked hand is at the right rear (45 degrees), and both left leg and left arm are turned towards the front. Face is turned due east.

(6) For the left arm, be sure that the "three tips," that is, the tips of toes, fingers and nose, face one another.

(7) The right foot, having turned inward 135 degrees, that is, after the turning of body, should follow the direction of left leg and be changed accordingly to 45 degrees, with the toes pointing to the southeast.

(8) Straighten head as if there were something on it and sink breath into abdomen. Otherwise, you will not be able to keep up your spirits.

(9) Be sure that you keep your strength reserved and complete.

Form 5   Raise Hands and Step Up

(1) Shift weight slightly to the rear through the changing of steps. Raise toes of left foot slightly away from floor with heel on the floor (Fig. 27). Then turn left foot inward (45 degrees) with movement of waist (Fig. 28). Following the direction of tiptoe, sit firmly on left leg (Fig. 29). At

Fig. 27

Fig. 28

<table>
<tr><td>Fig. 29</td><td>Fig. 30</td></tr>
</table>

Fig. 29

Fig. 30

this time, raise right heel slightly off the ground and change right leg into empty stance. At the same time, turn both arms inward and keep palms erect, with right arm in front and slightly higher and left arm behind and slightly lower. Both arms are so poised as if they are going to close inwards. (Fig. 30)

(2) After sitting firmly on left leg, gradually move body to the left. Raise right foot and take a step forward to land in front of left foot, with heel coming down on floor and toes slightly off the floor. Stretch right arm, and bend left arm until it is below right arm; both arms are closed inward. Face is turned due south. (Figs. 31-32)

(3) Turn both arms at the same time: turn right hand inward with palm facing downward, and turn left hand outward with palm facing upward. Place left hand below right forearm to form the posture of "pulling back". (Fig. 33)

(4) Follow the movement of waist, move both arms in a downward arc, with left arm taking the lead and right arm following it. Bend left arm from below upward and inward until it is above the right arm, with palm facing downward. Both arms are closed. (Fig. 34)

(5) Turn right foot inward, shift weight to the right and sit firmly on

Fig. 31

Fig. 32

Fig. 33

Fig. 34

right leg. Place left palm on the inside of right forearm near the waist, looking as if it is going to press forward. (Fig. 35)

Fig. 35

Points to remember:

(1) While turning left foot inward and shifting weight to the left and raising leg to step forward, turn body with the moving of the left foot. This should not be done too early, otherwise it will not be possible to coordinate the movements of the upper and lower parts of the body, keep a proper balance and remain steady while raising the leg.

(2) When closing the arms, see to it that the hands are led along by the arms and do not move independently, so that the closing of arms gives the feeling that the whole body is closed.

(3) After closing, both the postures of pulling back and pressing forward (Fig. 33-35) belong to the continuous actions of "Raise Hands and Step Up", not the transitional actions between "Raise Hands and Step Up" and "White Crane Spreads Its Wings".

(4) In Fig. 32, when stretching out the right leg, you should loosen right hip; otherwise, the hip will stick out and the upper part of body will incline to one side.

Form 6   White Crane Spreads Its Wings

Shift weight to the right and sit firmly on right leg. Gradually raise left foot from the floor and take a step forward. Change the direction of left foot from southeast to due east and form a left empty step with toes coming down on the floor. Bend right arm from inside outward, then from below upward and then move it past the front of chest and face until it is above the head, with palm facing outward and fingers pointing leftward to form an arc. Move left hand downward, past the front of abdomen and then in an arc to the side of left hip, with palm facing downward and fingers pointing to the front. Face is turned due east, with eyes looking straight ahead. (Figs. 36-37. Fig. 37 is the front view of Fig. 36)

Fig. 36   Fig. 37

Points to remember:

(1) Straighten head as if there were something on it; sink breath into abdomen. The right arm looks as if it is going to push up while the left arm appears to press down, thereby forming the posture of both arms pulling in opposite directions and making the whole body feel extended.

(2) Do not throw out chest or stick up hips. The toes of front foot are on the floor, but as they take an empty stance, they cannot sustain weight.

This is to avoid both legs sustaining weight at the same time, which may hamper flexibility of movement.

Form 7   Brush Knee and Twist Step (Left Style)

(1) While turning body slightly to the right with the waist leading, turn over both arms. Turn right arm inward, with palm facing obliquely upward, elbow down, and the tip of elbow sinking a little downward to form an arc; left arm is bent slightly inward from below upward, with palm bent obliquely downward to front of left hip. (Fig. 38)

(2) Following the lead of the waist, right arm continues to move in an arc from above downward until it is beside the right hip, shift weight gradually to the right; at the same time, left arm continues to bend from below upward. (Fig. 39)

(3) Continue to move right arm in an arc in the rear right direction (45 degrees) and then bend elbow, so as to make right forearm bend upward and gradually keep right palm erect. Meanwhile, bend left arm in an arc from above downward until it is bent in front of abdomen. Gradually sit firmly on right leg and change left leg into an empty stance. (Fig. 40)

Fig. 38

Fig. 39

Fig. 40   Fig. 41

(4) Stretch out left leg with heel landing first on the floor and toes lifted slightly off the floor. (Fig. 41)

(5) Move the four limbs following the lead of the waist. While turning body from right to left, move left arm and hand in an arc from the front of abdomen leftward and then forward, and then past knee until it is beside left knee, with fingertips pointing to the front; stretch right arm forward with palm erect. Shift weight gradually on to left leg, and bend left leg to form a left bow step. Face is turned due east, with eyes looking straight ahead. (Fig. 42)

Points to remember:

(1) From Fig. 38 to Fig. 42, move right arm in a downward and backward arc. Because the arc is large, pay attention to the angle and direction when turning the body. Right hand is at the right rear side (45 degrees).

(2) While bending right forearm upward in an arc, do not shrug shoulder or dangle elbow.

(3) When bending left arm inward, it moves basically in an upward arc. From Fig. 38 to Fig. 41, left arm moves in a semicircle (180 degrees).

(4) While turning body from right to left, see to it that the lower limbs

Fig. 42   Fig. 43

exert the straighening and sustaining strength so that the waist will lead the
four limbs to act at the same time and coordinate the movements of the upper and lower limbs.

(5) At the end of this form, see to it that the shoulders are relaxed; be
consciously aware whether they are straight or not. That is to say, avoid
sticking out right shoulder when stretching forward the right arm lest the
shoulders incline and the body not be in an erect position.

Form 8   Hand Strums the Lute

(1) With the waist leading, shift weight forward. First raise right heel,
then raise toes off the floor and sit firmly on left leg. (Fig. 43)

(2) Raise right foot and move it forward about the length of a fist before it lands on the floor. While turning body slightly to the right, shift
weight backward gradually and sit firmly on right leg. Stretch forward
left leg with heel landing on the floor and toes off the floor. Following
movement of waist, bend left arm from below upward, with palm facing
rightward. At the same time, move right arm from front to rear and withdraw it slightly downward until it comes to the inside of left arm, with
palm facing the left side. Face is turned due east, with eyes looking
straight ahead. (Fig. 44)

Fig. 44

Points to remember:

(1) While shifting weight, keep upper body erect and lower limbs steady.

(2) The movement of raising and withdrawing the two arms should follow the turning cf the waist. Do not shrug shoulders or dangle the elbows. When right palm is turned inward, it has the meaning of pressing, and when left palm is turned outward, it has the meaning of pushing.

Form 9   Brush Knee and Twist Step (Left Style)

(1) While turning waist slightly to the right, turn over both arms a bit. Left arm is bent from front upward and then downward until it is in front of chest, with palm facing downward; right arm is turned a little inward and moved in a downward arc until it is in front of right hip, with palm facing obliquely upward. Shift weight gradually on to right leg. (Figs. 45-46)

(2) Following the movement of the waist, the left arm continues to move in a downward arc from the front of chest to the front of abdomen. At the same time, right arm moves from the front of right hip in an upward arc, with forearm bent upward and right palm erect. Stretch out left leg with

57

Fig. 45   Fig. 46

toes coming down on floor first. Then, rest heel on floor, with toes raised. (Fig. 47)

(3) With the waist leading, turn body from right to left. Move left palm in an arc from front to the side of left knee, with palm facing downward; right arm is stretched out straight forward, with palm facing forward. At the same time, shift weight gradually forward, bend left leg to form a left bow step. Face is turned due east, with eyes looking straight ahead. (Fig. 48)

Points to remember:

(1) Though this form has the same name as Form 7, there are some differences in action between them because they follow behind different forms. In Form 7, because both arms, one upper and the other lower, are at the peak, the upper arm (right arm) has to be moved in a downward arc and the lower arm (left arm) has to be moved in an upward arc; while in Form 8, because both arms, one upper and the other lower too, are in the middle part, the upper arm (left arm) can still be moved upward and the lower arm (right arm) be moved downward.

(2) While right arm is moved in a downward and backward arc with body turned, it should be in the rear right direction (45 degrees).

58

Fig. 47   Fig. 48

(3) While moving right forearm in an arc and bending elbow upward, do not shrug shoulders or dangle the elbows.

(4) While turning body from right to left, be sure that the lower limbs exert the straightening and sustaining strength so that the waist will lead the four limbs to act at the same time and coordinate the movements of the upper and lower limbs.

(5) At the end of this form, see to it that the shoulders are relaxed and be consciously aware whether they are straight or not. That is to say, avoid sticking out right shoulder when stretching forward the right arm lest the shoulders incline and the body not be in an erect position.

Form 10   Brush Knee and Twist Step (Right Style)

(1) Shift weight slightly to the rear and, following the movement of the waist, turn over both palms slightly, with right palm facing obliquely leftward and left palm facing obliquely rightward. Raise left palm a little to the front of abdomen and with this movement turn left foot outward (45 degrees). (Fig. 49)

(2) Shift weight to the front, raise right heel first and then raise toes slowly. Bend right arm from front upward and then downward until it is in

Fig. 49   Fig. 50

front of abdomen; move left arm in an arc from the front of abdomen downward and then to rear left side (45 degrees). When left arm is moved nearly to the shoulder level, bend forearm upward with the palm erect. (Fig. 50)

(3) Sit firmly on left leg; raise right foot and take a step forward, with heel coming down on the floor and toes raised. (Fig. 51)

(4) Following the movement of the waist, move the four limbs and turn body from left to right. Bend right leg to form a right bow step. Move right hand in an arc from the front of chest to the front of abdomen, and then to the side of right knee, with palm facing downward and fingertips pointing to the front; stretch left arm straight forward, with palm facing forward. Face is turned due east, with eyes looking straight ahead. (Fig. 52)

Points to remember:

(1) While left arm is moved from below in an arc backward and upward, it should follow the turning of the body in the direction of the left rear (45 degrees).

(2) While bending left forearm in an arc upward, do not shrug the shoulders or dangle the elbows.

(3) While turning body from left to right, be sure that the lower limbs

| Fig. 51 | Fig. 52 |

exert the straightening and sustaining strength so that the waist will lead the four limbs to act at the same time and coordinate the movements of the upper and lower limbs.

(4) At the end of this form, see to it that the shoulders are relaxed, and be consciously aware whether they are straight or not. That is to say, avoid sticking out left shoulder while stretching forward the left arm so as to keep the shoulders straight and the body erect.

Form 11   Brush Knee and Twist Step (Left Style)

(1) Shift weight to the rear and, following the movement of the waist, turn over both palms slightly, with left palm facing obliquely rightward and right palm facing obliquely leftward. Raise right palm a little to the front of abdomen and with this movement turn right foot outward (45 degrees). (Fig. 53)

(2) While shifting weight to the front, first raise left heel and then raise toes slowly. Bend left arm from front upward and then downward until it is in front of abdomen; move right arm in an arc from the front of abdomen downward and then to rear right side (45 degrees). When right arm is

Fig. 53   Fig. 54

moved nearly to the shoulder level, bend forearm upward with the palm erect. (Fig. 54)

(3) Sit firmly on right leg; raise left foot and take a step forward, with heel coming down on the floor and toes raised. (Fig. 55)

(4) Following the movement of the waist, move the four limbs and turn body from right to left. Bend left leg to form a left bow step. Move left hand in an arc from the front of chest to the front of abdomen, and then to the side of left knee, with palm facing downward and fingertips pointing to the front; stretch right arm straight forward, with palm facing forward. Face is turned due east, with eyes looking straight ahead. (Fig. 56)

Points to remember:

The points are the same as those in Form 10, only the "right" and "left" positions are reversed.

Form 12   Hand Strums the Lute

The movements and points to remember are the same as those in Form 8. (Figs. 57-58)

Fig. 55

Fig. 56

Fig. 57

Fig. 58

Form 13   Brush Knee and Twist Step (Left Style)

The movements and points to remember are the same as those in Form 9. (Figs. 59-60-61)

Form 14   Step Up, Deflect Downward, Parry and Punch

(1) While shifting weight slightly to the rear, follow the movement of the waist and turn right arm inward, with palm facing obliquely leftward; raise left hand a little, with palm facing obliquely rightward, and with this movement turn left foot outward (45 degrees). Then, shift weight on to left leg and sit firmly on it in the direction of the tiptoes; gradually raise right heel and then toes off the floor. (Figs. 62-63)

(2) Raise right leg and take a step forward, with right toes turned outward (45 degrees); the step should not be too big. Following the movement of waist, move both arms in a downward arc from the front, with the left arm leading and the right arm following it. When they are moved to the rear left side (45 degrees) and are about to reach shoulder level, bend left forearm upward with the palm erect gradually; right hand is gradually changed from palm into fist, with wrist slightly erect and the back of fist

Fig. 59

Fig. 60

Fig. 61

Fig. 62

Fig. 63

stretched tight. (Fig. 64)

(3) Gradually shift weight to the right and slowly raise left foot off the floor. Follow the movement of waist and move both arms in an upward arc. Right fist moves with shifting of weight, with the back of fist stretched tight and the clutched fingers facing obliquely inward; meanwhile, along with movement of right fist, left arm waist for stretching forward with palm erect. (Fig. 65) (Figs. 66-67 are the front views.)

(4) Raise left leg and stretch it straight forward, with heel coming down on floor and toes raised. Stretch forward left palm and withdraw right fist to the side of right hip to form an arc with the clutched fingers facing upward. (Fig. 68)

(5) While shifting weight gradually on to left leg, bend left leg to form a left bow step. Turn right arm inward and stretch it forward with knuckles of fist facing the front. At the same time, withdraw left hand from the front to the place near the right elbow, with fingertips facing upward and palm rightward. The arms are shoulder-width apart. Face is turned due east, with eyes looking straight ahead. (Fig. 69)

Points to remember:

In this form, use right hand to deflect downward and left hand to

Fig. 64

Fig. 65

Fig. 66

Fig. 67

Fig. 68

Fig. 69

parry. Deflecting downward is again divided into sinking wrist and turning wrist. The movement towards the left is the former, and the movement towards the right is the latter. When the opponent's chest is exposed, you can hit it with a punch. Therefore, this form is called "Deflect Downward, Parry and Punch".

(2) As stretching the right foot forward is a transitional movement (Fig. 64), the stride should not be too big.

(3) As there are many continuous movements in this form, attention should be paid to their proper coordination.

(4) While clenching your fist, do not clench it too tight or too loose.

Form 15   Apparent Close-Up

(1) Bend left arm inward, with palm facing inward, and then turn palm upward and place it under right arm. Turn right arm from the front slightly to the left and change fist into palm, then shift weight to the rear. (Fig. 70)

(2) Gradually shift weight to the rear and sit firmly on right leg; turn body slightly to the right, withdraw right arm from the front to the place near the right part of the chest, with palm facing obliquely inward;

Fig. 70

with the elbow gradually sinking withdraw left arm from under right arm, to left part of chest, holding the hand erect with palm facing inward. (Fig. 71)

(3) Both arms follow the movement of waist as body turns from right to left. At the same time, follow the movement of arms, turn both palms forward, with palms facing the front. Shift weight from right leg on to left leg. (Fig. 72)

Fig. 71   Fig. 72

(4) Both arms follow the movement of waist and weight is shifted forward gradually. Bend left leg to form a left bow step. Meanwhile, push both arms straight forward. Face is turned due east, with eyes looking straight ahead. (Fig. 73)

Points to remember:

(1) While crossing arms and withdrawing right arm, do not keep right arm too close to the body, but should be about a fist away from armpit; be careful not to bend forward or lean backward, lest it hamper the turning of body.

(2) While pushing both arms forward, see to it that they follow the movement of waist; sink wrist with palms erect, and hold body erect, too.

Form 16   Cross Hands

(1) Turn both palms slightly inward to form an arc. Meanwhile, shift

Fig. 73   Fig. 74

weight to the rear gradually and turn body slightly to the right. (Fig. 74)

(2) Following the movement of waist, turn left foot inward (90 degrees), pointing due south. At the same time, move both arms from above downward and then in two different directions to the left and right side, with the right arm slightly in front and left arm behind it and both palms facing obliquely downward. Look ahead in the direction of right arm. (Fig. 75)

(3) After shifting weight from right leg on to left leg, sit firmly on left leg and change right leg into empty stance, with right heel slightly off the floor. Both arms continue to move in a downward arc, and with this movement turn both palms inward, with palms facing inward. (Fig. 76)

(4) After sitting firmly on left leg, turn right toes inward, then raise and draw them back to the right side of left foot, with feet shoulder-width apart and pointing straight ahead. As soon as right foot come down on floor, shift weight gradually on to right leg and sit firmly on it. At the same time, move both arms inward and cross both forearms to form an oblique cross in front of chest; both palms face inward, with the right palm on the outside. Face is turned due south, with eyes looking straight ahead. (Figs. 77-78)

Fig. 75

Fig. 76

Fig. 77

Fig. 78

Points to remember:

(1) While turing body to the right and moving both arms in a big arc, be sure that the right arm takes the lead and that the movements of the upper and lower limbs are well coordinated. While drawing right foot back and closing both arms inward, you should still hold both elbows down and stretch both forearms forward in a round form.

(2) While drawing right leg back, pay special attention to keeping the waist and hips relaxed. Do not stick out the hips or incline the body.

Form 17   Carry the Tiger to the Mountain

(1) While shifting weight slightly to the right, turn left foot inward, sit firmly on left leg and change right foot into empty stance. Move left arm in a downward arc until it is in front of abdomen; turn right arm inward to the front of chest, with palm facing obliquely downward. (Figs. 79-80)

Fig. 79   Fig. 80

(2) Continue to move left arm upward from below and when it is near the shoulder level, bend forearm with palm erect. Following the movement of waist, move right hand from above in a downward arc, past the chest, to the place in front of abdomen, with palm facing downward. Raise

72

right leg and stretch it forward with heel coming down on floor first. (Figs 81-82)

Fig. 81

Fig. 82

(3) Move the four limbs along with the waist. Move right hand in an arc from left to right, past the knee, until it comes to the side of right knee, with palm facing downward and fingers pointing forward; stretch left arm straight forward with palm facing forward. At the same time, following the movement of waist, bend right leg forward to form a right bow step. Face is turned to the northwest with eyes looking ahead. (Fig. 83)

Points to remember:

The points to remember are the same as those in Form 10.

This form also includes these three forms: "Pull Back", "Press Forward" and "Push". The movements and points to remember of these three forms are the same as the similar three forms in Form 3, except that the face is turned to the northwest. (Figs. 84, 85, 86, 87, 88, 89, 90)

Form 18   Fist Under Elbow

(1) The first movement is a transition from the last form to this one,

Fig. 83

Fig. 84

Fig. 85

Fig. 86

Fig. 87

Fig. 88

Fig. 89

Fig. 90

and it is performed basically in the same way as that in Form 4. (Figs. 91, 92, 93, 94)

(2) In Form 4, form right hand into hooked hand; while in this form, the right hand is not hooked, but the palm is kept erect. Turn left hand inward, with palm facing inward and left arm stretched tight. Change left foot into empty stance, with heel on floor and toes raised. Then following the movement of waist, gradually shift weight on to left leg, and raise right foot. With the movement of waist, turn both arms slightly to the left. (Figs. 95, 96, 97)

(3) Move the four limbs along with waist. Raise right leg and take half a step to the right, with toes coming down first on the floor and landing on the rear right side of left foot with toes pointing to the southeast. Following the movement of waist, turn both arms in an arc from right to left until the face is turned due east. Body is turned slightly to the right (45 degrees). (Fig. 98)

(4) Shift weight gradually on to right leg and change left leg into empty stance. Move left arm in an arc from above downward and just before it comes to the side of left hip, sink the elbow, bend the arm, and hoid the wrist erect. Then, move left arm in an arc from below upward until it is in

Fig. 91

Fig. 92

Fig. 93

Fig. 94

Fig. 95

Fig. 96

Fig. 97   Fig. 98

front of abdomen, with palm facing obliquely rightward and the part between thumb and index fingers a little upward. As the right hand moves from the right side, clench fist gradually, bend forearm with clenched fist inward. Sit firmly on right leg and stretch left leg with heel coming down on floor and toes raised. Raise left arm upward and forward, with palm facing rightward and the part between thumb and index finger upward; place right fist on the right lower side of left elbow. Face is turned due east and the body a little rightward (45 degrees), with eyes looking horizontally due east. (Figs. 99-100)

Points to remember:

(1) The essential point about turning is the same as Point (1) in Form 4.

(2) After the transition, while turning body to take half a step rightward, pay attention to the coordination of between upper and lower limbs and keep the upper part of body erect. While left arm is raised from below upward, it should be done as if it is raising an object and it should move in an arc. At the same time, while withdrawing right arm with clenched fist to the place below the left elbow, it should coordinate with the left arm and the speed should be even.

78

Fig. 99   Fig. 100

(3) The right fist should be bent inward with the clenched fingers facing leftward, making as if it going to hit the armpit of the opponent. Hold right elbow down so that the right arm is in a round form. Keep waist and hips relaxed, and keep chest and back in their natural positions.

Form 19   Step Back and Repulse the Monkey (Right Style)

(1) Change right fist into palm and move it downward to the side of right hip, with palm facing upward; turn left palm slightly inward. (Fig. 101)

(2) Move right arm in an arc backward. Just before right arm is raised to shoulder level, bend forearm with palm erect; turn left palm upward. The two palms are far apart facing each other, one in the front and the other in the rear. Sit firmly on right leg. (Fig. 102)

(3) Raise left leg and draw it backward, with toes coming down on floor and heel raised. Move left arm slightly backward and downward, and stretch right arm slightly forward from behind. (Fig. 103)

(4) Move the four limbs along the waist. When drawing the left foot backward, the toes come down on the floor first, then the inside of the foot

Fig. 101   Fig. 102

Fig. 103

lands on the floor, and finally the whole foot comes down on the floor and turns outward (45 degrees). Following the lead of the waist, shift weight on to left leg gradually and sit firmly on it; and with this movement turn right foot straight forward and place it in the front. Continue to withdraw left arm to the side of left hip to form an arc, with palm facing upward; continue to stretch right arm forward, with palm facing the front. Face is turned due east; body is turned slightly leftward (45 degrees), with eyes looking ahead. (Figs. 104-105)

| Fig. 104 | Fig. 105 |

Points to remember:

(1) The movement here requires you to step back, a movement which people are generally not accustomed to. Therefore, you should know where to place your foot, otherwise your posture might be wrong. It is advisable not to move the upper part of your body while stepping back so that you can straighten your left foot and step back in a straight line, and before it comes down on the floor, stretch it a little outward. Thus, the movement will be smooth when the weight is shifted on to left leg, and your posture will be correct. Remember, avoid by all means crossing your feet in confusion.

(2) There is the implied meaning of hitting when stretching the right arm forward with palm erect. Though in this form you retreat, there is in it the meaning of advancing to launch an attack. It is not suitable for the right wrist and right palm to be held in a loose and soft way.

(3) You are liable to stick out your hips while stepping back. Therefore you should guard against it.

Form 20   Step Back and Repulse the Monkey (Left Style)

Only one movement in this form is different from the one in the preceding form, that is, in the connection point with the form before it, the movement in Form 19 is to change right fist into palm and place it beside the right hip. All the other movements and points to remember in this form are the same as those in the preceding form, only reversing "right" and "left". (Figs. 106, 107, 108, 109, 110, 111)

Fig. 106   Fig. 107

Fig. 108

Fig. 109

Fig. 110

Fig. 111

Form 21   Step Back and Repulse
the Monkey (Right Style)

For the actions in this form, see Figs. 112, 113, 114, 115. The points

Fig. 112

Fig. 113

Fig. 114

Fig. 115

to remember are the same as those in the preceding form, only reversing "right" and "left".

Form 22   Slant Flying

(1) Move both arms in a downward arc with the left arm leading and the right arm following it. Left arm is moved first downward in an arc towards the left rear and then upward; just before it reaches the shoulder level, bend forearm inward to the upper part of the abdomen, with the palm facing downward. Right arm is moved towards the left to the lower part of the abdomen, with the palm turned upward. Both arms are closed. (Figs. 116-117. Fig. 117 is the side view.)

Fig. 116   Fig. 117

(2) After sitting firmly on left leg, raise right leg from the right rear (135 degrees) (in the southwest), and stretch it out with heel coming down on floor. (Figs. 118-119)

(3) Following the movement of waist, move the four limbs from left to right; along with this movement turn left foot inward. At the same time, shift weight on to right leg to form a right bow step. Both arms are separated with one on top of the other; place left hand in front of left hip, with palm turned slightly inward and facing downward; move right arm from

| Fig. 118 | Fig. 119 |

below upward and place it on the upper rear right side, with hand stretched and palm facing obliquely upward. Face is turned to the southwest, with eyes looking at right palm. (Fig. 120)

Points to remember:

(1) In this form, while turning body from left to right, it is not easy to control this movement because the angle is quite big (135 degrees). Therefore, it is necessary to keep weight on the left leg in the whole process, otherwise the body may lose its proper balance.

(2) The movement of turning left foot inward must follow the movement of the waist and coordinate it with the movement of separating the two arms, otherwise it will not be easy to turn.

(3) While turning body to the right (135 degrees) and stretching right leg out, be sure to keep the hips relaxed and the crotch in a round form. Do not stretch leg to the right rear alone without turning body.

(4) While moving right palm from below to the upper right side, relax and stretch the palm with wrist erect and fingers extended; don't let the palm sink.

Form 23   Raise Hands and Step Up

(1) While shifting weight forward, raise left foot a little off the floor

Fig. 120

and then turn it outward (45 degrees) and land on the floor. Then, gradually shift weight on to left leg and sit firmly on it; change right foot into empty stance with heel raised. Both arms are separated and moved in arcs to the left and right sides at the same time. (Figs. 121, 122, 123)

(2) After sitting firmly on left leg, stretch right leg out with heel coming down on floor and toes raised. At the same time, with weight shifted on to the left, both arms follow waist to close inward, with palms facing each other obliquely. Right arm is in front and slightly higher, and left arm is behind and slightly lower. Then, place left palm on the lower left side of right arm; bend right elbow with right palm erect and fingertips not higher than the level of eyebrow. Face is turned due south; body is turned slightly to the southeast, with eyes looking due south. (Figs. 124-125)

(3) See Figs. 126, 127, 128, 129.

Points to remember:

The points are the same as those in Form 5.

Form 24　　White Crane Spreads Its Wings

The movements and points to remember are the same as those in Form 6. For the movements see Fig. 130 and its front view Fig. 131.

Fig. 121   Fig. 122

Fig. 123

Fig. 124

Fig. 125

Fig. 126

Fig. 127

Fig. 128

Fig. 129

Fig. 130

Fig. 131

Form 25   Brush Knee and
Twist Step (Left Style)

The movements and points to remember are the same as those in Form 7. For the movements see Figs. 132, 133, 134, 135, 136.

Form 26   Needle at Sea Bottom

(1) While shifting weight forward, raise right foot and step forward about four inches. At the same time, bend right wrist downward. (Fig. 137)

(2) As soon as right foot comes down on floor, shift weight on to right leg, sit firmly on it and change left foot into empty stance. Both arms follow the waist as the body turns from left to right. Move right arm from the front in an upward arc to the right rear side, with palm facing the left side; at the same time raise left arm slightly upward. (Fig. 138)

(3) After sitting firmly on right leg, draw left leg a little inward with the toes coming down on floor to form an empty step. With body turned, bend waist and stretch right arm to the lower front side, with right palm facing leftward and fingertips pointing downward. At the same time, left palm

Fig. 132

Fig. 133

Fig. 134

Fig. 135

Fig. 136

Fig. 137

Fig. 138   Fig. 139

moves downward to the side of left hip, with palm facing downward and fingertips pointing forward. Face is turned due east, with eyes looking at the front of right palm. (Fig. 139).

Points to remember:

(1) In this form, the weight is as a whole on the right leg, but the left leg should coordinate with it mainly by loosening the left crotch.

(2) While moving right arm in an arc to the right, be careful not to shrug shoulder or dangle elbow, that is, the arc should not be too big.

(3) When turning body to the right, the upper part of body should not go beyond 45 degrees. While moving right arm in an upward and right-ward arc, it should have the meaning of rising in order to get ready for the next movement.

(4) Special attention should be paid not to stick out the hips, still less bend waist and head and look downward.

(5) Left arm should follow right arm in moving up and down, but the range of movement is smaller. Left arm should not remain still.

(6) In this form, the movement of waist is quite evident. Therefore, while turning body and bending waist, the four limbs must move along with

Fig. 140

the waist, otherwise the movements of the body, feet and hands will be disconnected and thrown into confusion.

Form 27 Fan Through the Back

(1) Raise the upper part of body and turn body slightly to the right. Right arm is gradually turned from below upward and from inside outward until it is raised to the shoulder level, with palm facing outward; left arm is bent inward, with the hand placed on the right wrist and palm facing outward. (Fig. 140)

(2) Raise left leg and stretch it forward to form a left bow step. At the same time, pull both arms apart, one in front and the other behind. Bend right elbow and raise right hand to the right side of the forehead; stretch left arm straight forward, with palm facing outward. Face is turned due east, with body turned slightly to the southeast and eyes looking straight ahead. (Fig. 141)

Points to remember:

(1) When you raise left foot and stretch it forward, see that it lands a little to the left so that the two feet will not be in a straight line while forming the left bow step.

Fig. 141

(2) While raising the upper part of body and stepping forward, sit firmly on right leg and don't stand up. While bending right elbow and placing right palm on the right side of the forehead, be sure to hold shoulder and elbow down, or else the movement of right arm will be disconnected with other parts.

Form 28　Chop Opponent with Fist

(1) Shift weight to the rear and, following the movement of the waist, turn body from left to the right rear and turn left foot inward (132 degrees); meanwhile, gradually shift weight on to left leg and sit firmly on it, with right foot changed to an empty stance. Bend left arm inward and place left hand by the side of the forehead, with palm facing outward; move right arm in an arc from above downward until it is between chest and abdomen; gradually keep wrist erect and clench fist with the knuckles facing upward. (Figs. 142, 143, 144)

(2) Following the movement of body, continue to turn the four limbs from left to right. Raise right foot and step forward (from due east to due west). At the same time, move left arm to the place beside the left rib, with its palm erect and facing obliquely forward; the right fist is first moved a

Fig. 142   Fig. 143

Fig. 144

little downward with the back of fist stretched tight, and then it is moved in an upward and forward arc to the front with the back of fist facing outward. (Fig. 145)

Fig. 145

(3) Shift weight to the right to form a right bow step. At the same time, draw back the right arm from the front in a downward arc to the place beside the right hip, with the clenched fingers facing upward; stretch the left arm forward. Face is turned due west, with eyes looking ahead. (Figs. 146-147. Fig. 147 is the front view.)

Points to remember:

(1) In this form, as there are many complex and continuous movements, care should be taken to ensure their coordination and continuity; the transition movements should not be regarded as fixed forms.

(2) In this form, you use the back of fist to hit the opponent; it has the same meaning as "Deflect Downward" in Form 14. Therefore, while clenching your fist, you should turn fist inward with the back of fist stretched tight so as to link the fits with the whole body organically. Other forms of clenching the fist are not suitable.

(3) In the course of turning the body, the angle of turning the foot in-

Fig. 146   Fig. 147

ward should be 135 degrees. If not, it will be difficult to stretch out the right leg and keep upper part of body in proper position. Therefore, the angle of turning foot plays an important role in providing a firm basis for keeping the body erect and coordinate it with the other parts. With a firm basis, you can move and turn naturally and with ease.

Form 29   Step Up, Deflect Downward, Parry and Punch

(1) While shifting weight to the left, change right leg into empty stance and turn body from right to left. Bend right elbow, clench right fist and, following the movement of waist, gradually move right arm from outside to inside and to the front until it comes to the left side, with clenched fingers facing obliquely downward; sink left elbow and bend left arm inward, With palm facing obliquely upward, and place it a little leftward below right arm. (Fig. 148-149)

For other movements, see Figs. 150, 151, 152, 153.

Points to remember:

The posture in Fig. 149 is the same as in Fig. 14 for the "Pull Back".

98

Fig. 148

Fig. 149

Fig. 150

Fig. 151

Fig. 152   Fig. 153

The only difference is that in Fig. 14 it is the palm and here it is the fist
that is involved. There should be the meaning of "Deflect Downward"
while moving the fist from right to left.

The other points are the same as those in Form 14.

Form 30   Step Up and
Grasp the Bird's Tail

(1) Shift weight slightly to the rear and, following the waist, turn body
to the left. Bend left arm and turn left hand outward, with palm facing
obliquely upward, then raise it to the left front side. At the same time,
change right fist into palm to face obliquely downward. (Fig. 154)

(2) Shift weight to the front and sit firmly on left leg; raise right
foot a little away from the floor. Move right arm in an arc downward and
inward and place it in front of abdomen. (Fig. 155)

(3) Stretch right leg forward to form a right bow step. Continue to
move right arm in an arc upward until it is below left arm and then stretch
it forward. Left arm is now placed at the lower left side of right arm, with
palm facing obliquely downward.

Fig. 154   Fig. 155

The following movements (Figs. 156, 157, 158, 159, 160, 161, 162, 163, 164) and point to remember are basically the same as those of "Ward Off Slantingly Upward", "Pull Back", "Press Forward" and "Push" in Form 3. There is only a little difference in the connecting parts which has been explained in Fig. 154 and in Fig. 155.

Points to remember:

There is a little difference in the connecting parts between this form and Form 3. In Form 3, there is the movement of "Ward Off Slantingly Upward" (left style), but in this form, this movement does not appear by itself, but is performed together with the movement of turning left arm outward (Fig. 154). So there is also the meaning of "Ward Off Slantingly Upward" in this form which embodies in "turning the arm". This point should not be ignored.

The other points are the same as those in Form 3.

Form 31   Single Whip

The movements and points to remember are the same as those in Form 4. (Figs. 165, 166, 167, 168, 169, 170, 171, 172)

Fig. 156

Fig. 157

Fig. 158

Fig. 159

Fig. 160

Fig. 161

Fig. 162

Fig. 163

Fig. 164

Fig. 165

Fig. 166

Fig. 167

Fig. 168

Fig. 169

Fig. 170

Fig. 171   Fig. 172

Form 32   Wave Hands Like
Clouds on Both Sides (1)

(1) Shift weight to the rear and, following the lead of the waist, turn body to the right, turn left foot inward (90 degrees); and bend left arm horizontally inward to the front of chest, with palm facing obliquely downward. (Fig. 173)

(2) Turn body from right to left until it faces the front and a little leftward; at the same time turn left arm inward with palm facing inward. While continuing to turn body slightly leftward, move left hand to the place in front of the left part of chest; the right hooked hand is changed into palm and is moved in a downward arc to the front of abdomen. Shift weight gradually to the left. (Fig. 174)

(3) While continuing to turn body to the left, shift weight on to left leg and change right foot into empty stance. Left arm is turned from right to left and from inside to outside, with palm facing obliquely outward; right hand is moved from below upward until it is in front of chest. (Figs. 175, 176, 177)

(4) Raise right foot and draw it half a step leftward and land on the

Fig. 173   Fig. 174

Fig. 175

Fig. 177

floor, with toes pointing forward. Shift weight gradually to the right and turn body rightward to face the front. Move right arm in an arc until it is in front of the right part of chest; the left arm is also moved in an arc until it comes to the left front side of abdomen, with both palms facing inward. (Figs. 178-179)

Form 33   Wave Hands Like
Clouds on Both Sides (2)

(1) Continue to turn body rightward (about 45 degrees). Following the movement of body, turn right arm gradually outward, with palm facing obliquely downward; left arm is moved from below upward little by little until it is in front of abdomen. Shift weight gradually on to right leg and sit firmly on it; raise left heel to form an empty step. (Fig. 180)

(2) After sitting firmly on right leg, raise left foot and stretch it to the left side, with the inside of foot coming down first and then the whole foot on the floor. (Fig. 181)

(3) As soon as left foot comes down on floor, the whole body, with the waist leading, turns from right to left, then sit gradually and firmly on left

Fig. 178

Fig. 179

Fig. 180

Fig. 181

leg and draw right leg towards left leg, with both feet now shoulder-width apart. At the same time, continue to move both arms in an arc and when the body is turned to the straight front, the right arm has moved in an arc to the place in front of the right part of chest, and the left arm has moved in an arc to the place in front of the right part of abdomen; both palms are now facing inward. (Figs. 182-183)

Fig. 182

Fig. 183

(4) Continue to turn body to the left side (45 degrees) and shift weight gradually to the right. Move both arms in an arc to the left side, with the two palms facing each other. Then, from left to right, move both arms, with one above the other, in an arc past the straight front side to the right side (45 degrees), and both palms meet again and face each other. At this time, sit firmly on right leg and raise left heel to form an empty stance; together with the movement of body, the head also turns without slackening. (Figs. 184, 185, 186)

Form 34   Wave Hands Like Clouds on Both Sides (3)

(1) After sitting firmly on right leg, immediately stretch left leg to the left side, and as soon as the left foot comes down on floor, turn body

Fig. 184

Fig. 185

Fig. 186

from right to the left side (45 degrees) and shift weight on to left leg. Both arms continue to move in an arc, turn left arm from inside upward and outward, with palm facing outward to the left side; move right arm from below upward, with palm facing inward. (Figs. 187-188)

Fig. 187   Fig. 188

(2) When sitting firmly on left leg, draw right leg inward, with toes turned inward in order to get ready for a measured gait with toes pointing outward in the next form. Both arms continue to move in an arc, the left arm moving downward and the right arm upward. Just before the two arms move to the shoulder level, they meet on the left side again. (Fig. 189)

(3) Following the movement of waist, turn the whole body from the right side (45 degrees). Shift weight on to right leg and sit firmly on it, change left leg into an empty stance with heel raised. Following the body, both arms continue to move in an arc up and down, the right arm moving from inside outward and the left arm from outside inward. Both arms meet on the right side.

Points to remember:

(1) With the waist leading the movements, turn to the left and right sides to wave hands. See that the movements of the four limbs are led by

112

Fig. 189

the waist; be sure to turn them slowly and coordinate the movement of the upper limbs with that of the lower limbs.

(2) The two arms are turned upward and downward and to the left and right sides. While turning the arms leftward, the left arm take the lead and the right arm follows; while turning them rightward, the right arm takes the lead and the left arm follows. The movement of the hand that leads from below upward has the meaning of "Ward Off Slantingly Upward". When the hand that leads is turned sideways, the palm is gradually turned from inside outward, while the other arm moves accordingly from outside gradually inward, with the two moving in alternation.

(3) The movements of waving hands are divided into the left and right sides, that is, upward and downward, and this constitutes one form of "Wave Hands Like Clouds on Both Sides". Generally, three such forms are performed continuously one after the other, just as in "Brush Knee and Twist Step", "Step Back and Repulse the Monkey" and "Part the Wild Horse's Mane" when three forms are performed continuously one after the other. You can also do five such forms continuously, but remember it must be in odd numbers, not in even numbers, so as to suit the requirements of the arrangement of this series.

(4) When raising foot and stretching it sideways to the left, or placing right foot to the left side, you should always turn toes inward, with the toes first, then the inner side of the sole and lastly the whole foot coming down on floor. You must sit firmly on one leg before raising the other leg. Be careful to maintain the same level and keep a proper balance.

(5) As stated above, you should use the waist to lead the movement of the four limbs, turn them smoothly to the left and right sides and coordinate the movement of the upper and lower limbs. There are some trainees, however, who only turn their hands without moving the waist, as if the hands have no connection with the arms and other parts of the body. If you should do so, your hands will not be able to move with ease, your body will be stiff and your steps will fall into confusion.

(6) In the course of turning, see that the waist and hips are relaxed, otherwise the hips will stick out.

Form 35   Single Whip

(1) When the two arms meet at the end of the preceding form, the right hand at once turns into a hooked hand, the left palm is moved to face inward and the head follows the movement of the body, and the face is turned towards the right side. (Fig. 190)

Fig. 190

(2) Stretch left leg to the left front side, with heel coming down on floor. With the waist leading, move the four limbs from right to left and bend left leg to form a left bow step; meanwhile, from the place in front of the chest, the left arm is turned outward and is gradually stretched forward, with palm facing outward. Face is turned due east and the right hand points to the southwest, eyes looking due east. (Figs. 191-192)

Fig. 191

Fig. 192

Points to remember:

The points are the same as those in Form 4.

Form 36   High Pat on Horse

(1) While turning body from left to right, shift weight gradually on to right leg and sit firmly on it; raise left foot slightly off the floor. At the same time, change right hooked hand into palm and stretch it forward, with palm facing downward. Then, as the right arm bends inward, bend the hand from the rear to the place in front of the chest; at the same time, left palm follows left arm from the front and turns inward, with palm facing obliquely upward. (Fig. 193-194)

(2) Following the movement of waist, both arms are moved from right

| Fig. 193 | Fig. 194 |

to left and body is turned to face the front. From the place in front of the chest, the right palm is stretched upward and forward, with palm turned inward and facing downward; at the same time, bend left arm and move left elbow backward to withdraw left palm to the place in front of the left part of waist, with palm facing obliquely upward and fingers pointing obliquely forward. At the same time, raise left foot and move it rightward to land in the front and form an empty stance, with toes on floor and heel raised. Face is turned due east, with eyes looking ahead. (Fig. 195)

Points to remember:

(1) When shifting weight to the right, you must turn the body to the right at the same time, and sit firmly on right leg. In doing so, you can raise the left leg naturally and easily. If you do not turn the body, you will find it difficult to raise the leg and your body cannot remain steady.

(2) "High Pat on Horse" is to stretch forward the right palm with its edge pointing to the front to hit the opponent. Therefore, see that the right hand is bent inward with wrist erect, and the fingers are not pointing towards the front, but a little to the left.

(3) "High Pat on Horse" is a higher posture with a left empty step. As the right arm stretches forward, the upper part of the body also moves

116

Fig. 195

Fig. 196

a little forward and upward, but take care not to incline the body forward. The stretched right hand is a little bit higher and is on a level with the eyebrow.

Form 37   Separation of Right Foot

(1) With the waist taking the lead, move the four limbs and turn body rightward. After shifting weight on to the right, sit firmly on right leg and change left foot into an empty stance. Both arms are moved in an arc at the same time. Right arm is moved from the front rightward and backward until it is in front of chest, with palm facing downward; left arm is moved in an arc from inside outward and forward, with palm facing obliquely upward. The two palms face each other. (Fig. 196)

(2) Continue to move both arms in an arc; right arm is moved backward and left one forward. At the same time, stretch left foot out to the left side (45 degrees) in the northeast direction, with heel coming down on floor and toes raised. (Figs. 197-198)

(3) Shift weight gradually to the left to form a left bow step. Continue to move both arms in an arc. Right arm is moved half stretched to the right

Fig. 197   Fig. 198

side, with palm facing obliquely downward; left arm is placed in front of
abdomen, with palm facing obliquely inward. (Fig. 199).

(4) Turn body from right to the left side (45 degrees), that is, in the direction of the toes. Then, shift weight forward again and raise right foot
gradually off the floor. Following the waist, pull both arms to the left side (45
degrees) to form an oblique cross, with the left palm on the inside and the
right palm on the outside; both palms face inward. (Fig. 200)

(5) While shifting weight forward again, stand up on left leg and raise
right leg with instep stretched tight. The two arms are turned to the left and
right sides, with the palms gradually turned outward. Body is turned towards
the southeast direction. (Figs 201-202)

(6) Right foot kicks towards the right side, with the instep straightened. At the same time, stretched both arms and separate them to the left and
right sides, with both palms facing outward. Face is turned to the southeast,
with eyes looking to the front in the southeast direction. (Fig. 203)

Points to remember:

(1) Each of the two arms move in a circle separately. Right arm is
moved from inside outward and then inward again. In the course of moving
in an arc, both arms are moved horizontally, and the upper arm is always on

Fig. 199

Fig. 200

Fig. 201

Fig. 202

Fig. 203

the top while the lower arm is always below, and this position should not be changed. After moving in an arc, the two arms are in a position of pulling. Note that the body inclines to the right side, and knees and elbows are opposite to each other.

(2) Note the direction of both oblique angles. While moving the arms round to do the pulling action, turn face to the right oblique angle and pull arms to the left side; while both hands are crossed, body is turned towards the left oblique angle; while kicking with right foot, body is again turned towards the right oblique angle.

(3) The pulling action should follow the lead of the waist, especially the upper limbs. See that the back follows the movement of the waist, and the arms follow the movement of the back, and the wrists and hands should move along with the back and arms. You should not turn the wrists only as if they have no connections with the arms. If this should happen, then the movements are not led by the waist.

(4) When standing up on the left leg, the left leg seems to be straight but not actually so. That is to say, it is not quite straight, nor should you bend it too much.

(5) With regard to the direction of arms, the right arm is in the same

direction as the right leg, and the left arm is placed to the left rear (135 degrees).

Form 38   Separation of Left Foot

(1) Bend left arm inward to the front of the chest, with palm facing obliquely downward; turn right arm inward at the same time, with palm facing obliquely upward. Both palms which are apart face each other. Bend right leg. (Fig. 204)

(2) Bend left leg and lower right leg to let it fall with the heel coming down on floor and toes raised, pointing to the southeast. At the same time, move both arms in an arc, the right arm is moved from front leftward and inward while the left arm is moved from inside rightward and forward. (Fig. 205)

Fig. 204   Fig. 205

(3) Bend right leg. Continue to move both arms in an arc to both sides, forming left and right pulling positions. (Fig. 206)

(4) Turn body from left to right. With the waist taking the lead, pull both arms to the right side. Then, after shifting weight on to right leg, raise left foot from the floor, and put right arm on top of left arm to form an oblique cross. (Fig. 207)

Fig. 206   Fig. 207

(5) While shifting weight forward, stand up on right leg and raise left leg with instep stretched tight. Turn the two arms to the left and right sides, with palms turned outward. Body is turned towards the northeast. (Figs. 208-209)

(6) Left foot kicks towards the left side, with instep straightened. At the same time, stretch both arms and move them to left and right sides, with the two palms facing outward. Face is turned to the northeast, with eyes looking at the front in the northeast direction. (Fig. 210)

Points to remember:

The points are the same as those in the preceding form, only reversing "right" and "left".

Form 39   Turn and Kick with Left Heel

(1) Left leg is bent downward, with toes pointing downward. (Fig. 211)

(2) Both arms are turned inward, with palms facing inward. (Fig. 212)

(3) With right heel as the axis, turn body to the left rear (135 degrees), from the northeast to due west; keep the left leg bent, with toes

Fig. 208

Fig. 210

Fig. 209

Fig. 211

pointing downward. At the same time, close both arms in front of chest and cross them with the left arm on the outside and the right arm inside and both palms facing inward. (Fig. 213)

Fig. 212   Fig. 213

(4) Separate the arms towards two sides. Left arm points in the direction of due west, with palm facing outward; right arm points in the direction of northeast, with palm facing obliquely outward. At the same time, left heel kicks forward, with toes pointing upward. Face is turned due west, with eyes looking straight forward. (Fig. 214)

Points to remember:

(1) While turning bcdy from right to left, take right heel as the axis. This is because the empty stance and solid stance are not changod though the direction is changed. Use the waist to coordinate the balance of the upper and lower limbs, because the waist dominates the movement of the whole body.

(2) While kicking left heel forward, be sure to keep the toes upward. The main point of kicking left heel forward is basically the same as the separation of left foot. The only difference is that in the former action you keep the toes upward, while in the latter case, the toes point forward, with instep straightened.

Fig. 214

Form 40   Brush knee
and Twist Step (Left Style)

(1) Right leg is bent a little forward and left leg falls with heel coming down on floor first. Right arm is turned inward, with palm facing obliquely upward; the right arm is then moved in a downward and backward arc. Just before the right arm is raised to the shoulder level, bend its forearm upward, with palm erect; left arm is then bent to the place in front of abdomen. (Figs. 215-216)

(2) With the waist leading, move the four limbs, turn the body from right to left and shift weight leftward to form a left bow step. At the same time, move both arms in an arc; the left arm moves past left knee and then to its left side, with palm facing downward and fingers pointing forward; the right palm is stretched forward with palm facing forward. Face is turned due west, with eyes looking straight ahead. (Figs. 217-218)

Fig. 215

Fig. 216

Fig. 217

Fig. 218

Points to remember:

The points are the same as those in Form 7.

Form 41   Brush Knee and
Twist Step (Right Style)

The movements (Figs. 219, 220, 221, 222) and points to remember in this form are the same as those in Form 10.

The movements in Form 9 and Form 10 are performed with the face turned to the east, while in Form 40 and Form 41, the face is turned to the west. Therefore, in Form 9 and Form 10, you can only see the action of moving in arcs on the right but not the actions on the left; but in Form 40 and Form 41, the movements are performed with the face turned to the west, and therefore you can see the action on the left.

Form 42   Step Up and Punch Downward

(1) While shifting weight slightly backward, turn right foot outward (45 degrees), and gradually shift weight on to right leg. Turn right arm outward and change the hand gradually into fist to place it in front of right hip, with knuckles facing downward; bend left arm slightly inward, with palm facing downward. (Fig. 223)

Fig. 219   Fig. 220

Fig. 221

Fig. 222

Fig. 223

(2) Shift weight forward and sit firmly on right leg. Raise left foot and stretch it forward, with heel coming down first on the floor and toes raised. At the same time, turn body to the right, place right fist at the side of right hip; continue to bend left arm inward and place it in front of abdomen. (Figs. 224-225)

Fig. 224

Fig. 225

(3) With the waist taking the lead, move the four limbs, turn the body from right to left, and shift weight gradually on to left leg to form a left bow step. Move both arms forward in an arc at the same time; the left hand is moved past the knee and placed at the side of left knee, with palm facing downward and fingers pointing forward; from the side of right hip, the right fist is turned inward, with the clenched fingers facing leftward. Then, bend waist and hit towards the lower front side with the right fist. Face is turned towards the lower front side of right fist. (Figs. 226-227)

Points to remember:

(1) The transitional movements of the left arm in this form are the same as those in Form 40, but here the right hand is to clench the fist and hit towards the lower front side with the waist bent.

(2) "Punch Downward" is to hit towards the lower front side. Be sure

Fig. 226   Fig. 227

to keep waist and hips relaxed lest you should stick out the hips. Do not drop your head to look downward.

Form 43   Turn Over and
Chop Opponent with Fist

(1) Shift weight backward and raise the upper part of body. With the waist taking the lead, turn body to the right. At the same time, turn left foot inward (135 degrees) and sit firmly on it; change right foot into empty stance. Left arm is bent from below upward until it is beside the left side of the forehead, with palm facing outward; raise right fist and bend right elbow to form an arc and place right fist between the chest and abdomen, with the clenched fingers facing downward, wrist erect and fist bent a little upward. (Fig. 228)

Movement (2) and movement (3) are the same as movement (1), movement (2) and movement (3) in Form 28; the only difference is that they are performed in an opposite direction. (Figs. 229-230)

Fig. 228

Fig. 229

Fig. 230

Points to remember:

The points are the same as those in Form 28.

Form 44   Step Up, Deflect
Downward, Parry and Punch

The movements and points to remember are the same as those in Form 29; the only difference is that the movements are performed in an opposite direction. In the transition from Form 28 to Form 29, the face is turned towards the west; now from Form 43 to Form 44, the face is turned towards the east. Please see Figs 231, 232, 233 , 234, 235, 236, 237, 238, and you will get a clearer idea.

Form 45   Kick with Heel

(1) Shift weight slightly backward and turn left foot leftward (45 degrees). While turning body to the left, shift weight gradually on to left leg, sit firmly on it and raise right foot a little away from the floor. At the same time, turn left arm slightly inward, with palm facing obliquely inward; right fist is changed into palm and is moved first in a downward and then upward arc, with arm turned inward and palm facing inward. Both hands are placed in front of chest to form a cross, with the right arm on the outside

Fig. 231

Fig. 232

Fig. 233

Fig. 234

Fig. 235

Fig. 236

Fig. 237   Fig. 238

and the left arm inside. Raise right foot and place it by the side of left foot to form an empty step. Eyes look ahead. (Figs. 239-240)

(2) Arms are separated to both sides, with palms turned outward. At the same time, right heel kicks forward, with toes pointing up; while kicking right heel forward, stand up straight on left leg. Face is turned due east, with eyes looking straight ahead. (Figs. 241-242)

Points to remember:

The points are the same as those in Form 39, only the movements are in the opposite direction and you have to reverse "right" and "left". As to the direction of the arms, the right arm is in the due east direction and left arm in the northwest direction.

Form 46   Hit the Tiger (Left Style)

(1) Bend right leg, with toes pointing slightly downward. (Fig. 243)

(2) Left leg is bent a bit as right foot falls on floor, with toes turned a little inward and heel coming down on floor. Bend left arm and turn palm gradually inward. (Fig. 244)

134

Fig. 239

Fig. 240

Fig. 241

Fig. 242

Fig. 243   Fig. 244

(3) Shift weight gradually on to right leg and sit firmly on it; change left leg into empty stance. Left arm is placed below right arm near the elbow, with palm facing obliquely inward. (Fig. 245)

(4) Raise left leg and stretch it to the left front side. After left heel comes down on floor, move the four limbs along with the waist from right to left and shift weight gradually on to left leg to form a left bow step. From right to left, left arm is turned first downward and then upward, with palm gradually turned outward; the left hand gradually clenches the fist and moves to the upper front part of the left forehead. At the same time, the right arm follows left arm and moves in a downward arc to the front of the abdomen; right hand gradually clenches the fist, with the clenched fingers facing inward. Face is turned towards the front of the left side, and eyes look straight ahead. (Figs. 246-247) (Fig. 247 is the front view.)

Points to remember:

(1) Right foot falls on floor naturally as left leg is bent a bit, so that the action will not be stiff.

(2) In this form, while moving the arms in arcs, try to move them as round as possible. For this reason, both arms should move in coordination with the movement of waist. At the end of this form, the arc shown by both

Fig. 245

Fig. 246

Fig. 247

arms should also be round with the left arm above the left side of the forehead and the right arm in front of abdomen.

(3) From Fig. 244 to Fig. 245, the movements done by both arms are to finish the pulling pose gradually. Therefore, it is necessary to pay attention to the position of left arm, that is to say, the action of pulling should be completed on the right side.

(4) Owing to technical reasons, the photographs do not show the continuity of some movements. It is therefore necessary to read the explanations carefully.

(5) In this form, the bow step is a little like the posture of riding a horse obliquely, and is therefore different from the normal bow steps.

Form 47　　Hit the Tiger (Right Style)

(1) Shift weight backward and, with the waist leading, turn left foot inward. (Fig. 248)

(2) While turning left foot inward (90 degrees), shift weight gradually on to left leg, and the body has basically turned from the left front to the right side. Meanwhile, the weight has been shifted on to left leg, then change

Fig. 248

right leg into empty stance. Loosen both fists into palms and they form the pulling posture on the left side. (Fig. 249)

(3) With the waist leading, moving the four limbs, turn the body from left to right and bend right leg gradually to form a right bow step. Both arms move at the same time in a downward arc, with the right arm leading and the left arm following it. Right arm is moved from the left downward past the abdomen and then turned outward and upward; the palm is gradually changed into fist as it comes to the upper part in front of the right side of the forehead, with the clenched fingers facing outward; move left arm in an arc to the front of abdomen and change palm into fist, with the clenched fingers facing inward. Face is turned towards the front right side, with the eyes looking straight ahead. (Fig. 250)

Fig. 249

Fig. 250

Points to remember:

The points are the same as those in the preceding form, only reversing "right" and "left".

Form 48   Turn and Kick with Right Heel

(1) With the waist leading, move the four limbs, turn body from right to

left and sit firmly on left leg. Following the waist, both arms are moved from right to left; the left arm is moved from below in a leftward and upward arc until it is in front of left chest; the right arm is moved in a downward and then upward arc until it touches the left arm to form an oblique cross, with both palms facing inward and eyes looking due east. (Figs. 251-252)

Fig. 251   Fig. 252

(2) Stand up on left leg, raise right leg and kick straight forward with the right heel. At the same time, both fists are gradually changed into palms; then they separate and move to both sides, with palms facing obliquely outward, right arm pointing due east and left arm pointing to the northwest. Eyes look due east. (Figs. 253-254)

Points to remember:

The points are the same as those in Form 45.

Form 49   Strike Opponent's
Ears with Both Fists

(1) Bend right leg downward naturally with toes pointing downward. (Fig. 255)

Fig. 253

Fig. 254

Fig. 255

(2) With the waist leading, turn body to the right (45 degrees) and at the same time turn right toes outward (45 degrees). Bend left arm from left to right until it comes to the place obliquely above the right leg, with palm facing obliquely upward; turn right arm inward, with palm also facing obliquely upward. The palms are shoulder-width apart and are placed over both sides of the right leg. (Figs 256-257)

Fig. 256

Fig. 257

(3) Left leg is bent a little downward as the right leg falls with its heel coming down first on floor and the toes raised. At the same time, with the elbows bent, move both arms from the front downward and backward to both sides of the ribs, with palms facing obliquely upward. (Figs. 258-259)

(4) Shift weight forward gradually and bend right leg to form a right bow step. Both palms are gradually turned from inside outward and moved in a forward and upward arc and then changed into fists to hit the ears of the opponent. Face is turned towards the southeast, with eyes looking straight ahead. (Fig. 260)

Points to remember:

(1) While turning body rightward, with the waist leading, turn right foot outward. As the right leg does not change its empty or solid stance, but

Fig. 258

Fig. 259

Fig. 260

there is only a change of direction, you should therefore take right heel as the axis while turning.

(2) While moving the four limbs up and down, be sure to coordinate the movement of the upper and lower limbs, especially the movement of turning the body (from Fig. 255 to Fig. 256). Though the angle of this movement is not very big, if you don't take care to coordinate the movement of the upper and lower limbs, the upper part of the body may not be able to remain steady.

(3) While hitting outward, both arms should move in arcs, that is, both arms should move in a round way and the hands should be changed nimbly.

Form 50   Kick with Left Heel

(1) Shift weight gradually on to right leg and raise left foot off the floor. Move both arms from above to left and right sides and then downward to the place in front of the chest to form an obligue cross, with the left arm on the outside and the clenched fingers of both hands facing inward. (Figs. 261-262)

(2) Stand up on right leg, raise left leg and kick straight forward. Both arms are separated to both sides and fists are changed into palms, with left leg and left arm pointing due east, right arm pointing to the southwest, and

Fig. 261   Fig. 262

both palms facing outward. Face is turned due east, with eyes looking straight ahead. (Figs. 263-264)

Fig. 263

Fig. 264

Points to remember:

The points are the same as those in Form 39.

Form 51   Turn and Kick with Right Heel

(1) Left leg is bent downward naturally with toes pointing downward. (Fig. 265)

(2) Stretch left leg forward. Left arm is bent slightly inward, with palm facing inward; right arm is moved in a downward arc, with palm facing obliquely downward. (Fig. 266)

(3) With the waist leading, move the four limbs; with the right sole as the axis, turn left foot inward from left to right (315 degrees) and then let it come down on floor with toes pointing to the northeast. Sit firmly on left leg and change right foot into empty stance. Move both arms at the same time in arcs from left to right. (Figs. 267-268)

(4) Bend both arms and form an oblique cross on the left side, with the right arm on the outside and both palms facing inward. Stand up on left

145

Fig. 265

Fig. 266

Fig. 267

Fig. 268

leg, raise right leg and kick outward with the right heel. Turn both arms outward at the same time and separate them to both sides, with palms facing obliquely outward, right arm pointing due east and left arm pointing to the northeast. Face is turned due east, with eyes looking straight ahead. (Figs. 269-270)

Fig 269   Fig. 270

Points to remember:

(1) In this form, the angle of turning the body is quite big (315 degrees), it is therefore necessary to coordinate the movements of the upper and lower limbs. That is to say, the turning of body, the falling of leg, the closing of arms, the raising of leg, the kicking out of heel and the separation of arms — all these actions should be well coordinated and the speed of movement should be appropriate.

(2) Though the angle of turning the body is quite big, the direction remains the same, and the empty and solid stances have been interchanged. Right leg is changed from empty stance to solid stance and left leg from solid stance to empty stance, so you should take right toes as the axis in turning. If the empty and solid stances are interchanged, take the toes as the axis; otherwise take the heel as the axis.

147

Form 52   Step Up, Deflect
Downward, Parry and Punch

(1) Bend right leg downward naturally. (Fig. 271)

(2) While bending left leg slightly, turn right toes outward (45 degrees) and pointing to the southeast, then it falls on floor. Left arm is on the left side, with palm erect. (Fig. 272)

Fig. 271

Fig. 272

(3) Shift weight gradually on to right leg and raise left foot. Turn right arm inward, clench fist and deflect it downward to the side of right hip; meanwhile, stretch left palm straight forward. (Fig. 273)

(4) With the waist leading, move the four limbs, sit firmly on right leg, raise left leg and stretch it straight forward to form a left bow step. Turn right fist inward, with the knuckles of fist pointing to the front, and then hit straight forward; left arm is withdrawn to the left side of right elbow, with palm facing rightward and fingers pointing upward. Face is turned due east, with eyes looking straight ahead. (Figs. 274-275)

Points to remember:

The points are the same as those in Form 14, only in this form, turn the

Fig. 273

Fig. 274

Fig. 275

149

body directly to the right, clench right fist and turn wrist directly to deflect rightward, without sinking wrist to deflect leftward.

Form 53   Apparent Close-Up

The movements and points to remember are the same as those in Form 15. (Figs. 276, 277, 278, 279, 280)

Fig. 276

Fig. 277

Form 54   Cross Hands

The movements and points to remember are the same as those in Form 16. (Figs. 281, 282, 283, 284)

Form 55   Carry the
Tiger to the Mountain

The movements and points to remember are the same as those in Form 17. (Figs. 285, 286, 287, 288, 289, 290, 291, 292, 293, 294)

Form 56   Diagonal Single Whip

The movements and points to remember are the same as those in Form 4; the only difference is that the movements are performed in the opposite

150

Fig. 278

Fig. 279

Fig. 280

Fig. 281

Fig. 282

Fig. 283

Fig. 284

Fig. 285

Fig. 286

Fig. 287

Fig. 288

Fig. 289

Fig. 290

Fig. 291

Fig. 292

Fig. 293   Fig. 294

direction. At the end of Form 4, the face is turned due east, while in this form, the face is turned to the southeast. (Figs. 295, 296, 297, 298, 299, 300, 301)

Form 57   Part the Wild Horse's Mane (Right Style)

(1) Shift weight backward and, following the movement of the waist, turn left foot inward (90 degrees) and body rightward (90 degrees). At the same time, turn both arms rightward (90 degrees), too (Fig. 302)

(2) After shifting weight gradually on to left leg, raise right leg and stretch it slightly forward to the right, with heel coming down first on floor and toes raised. Then, while shifting weight backward, change right hooked hand into palm and turn right arm inward from front to rear until right palm is under left arm, with the palm facing obliquely upward. Both palms are obliquely opposite each other. (Figs. 303-304)

(3) Move the four limbs along with the waist, turn the body from left to right, shift weight gradually on to right leg and bend it to form a right bow step. At the same time, both arms are separated; the left arm moves

155

Fig. 295

Fig. 296

Fig. 297

Fig. 298

Fig. 299

Fig. 300

Fig. 301

Fig. 302

Fig. 303

Fig. 304

downward and the left palm is placed beside left hip, with palm facing obliquely downward; the right arm moves upward and the right palm is moved from below upward and then towards the upper right side, with palm facing obliquely upward until it is level with eyebrow. Face is turned towards the front, a little to the right side, and eyes look at the front of right arm. (Fig. 305)

Fig. 305

Form 58   Part the Wild Horse's Mane (Left Style)

(1) Shift weight slightly backward and, with the waist leading, turn right foot a little rightward and shift weight instantly on to right leg and change left foot into an empty step. At the same time, left arm is gradually bent from below upward and from left to right until its palm is under right arm, with palm facing obliquely upward; right arm is turned a little inward, with palm facing obliquely downward. Both arms are closed. (Figs. 306-307)

(2) Raise left foot and stretch it forward slightly to the left, with heel coming down on floor and toes raised. (Fig. 308)

(3) Move the four limbs along with the waist. Turn body from right to

Fig. 306

Fig. 307

Fig. 308

left, shift weight gradually on to left leg and bend it to form a left bow step. Both arms are separated, one upward and the other downward; right palm is placed beside right hip, while the left arm turns from below upward, and left palm moves towards the upper left side with palm facing obliquely upward until it is level with eyebrow. Face is turned towards the front, a little to left, and eyes look at the front of left forearm. (Fig. 309)

Fig. 309

Form 59   Part the Wild Horse's Mane (Right Style)

The movements are the same as those in the preceding form, only reversing "right" and "left." (Figs 310,311, 312, 313, 314)

Points to remember:

(1) The movements in this form are similar to those in Form 22, but the range of turning is smaller than that in Form 22. Though the forearm is used to attack the opposing party in both forms, the methods are different.

(2) In this form the direction is due front, a little inclined to the left, so the angle should be less than 45 degrees while changing the steps.

(3) Because in turning the body the distance is short and the range is

Fig. 310

Fig. 311

Fig 312

Fig. 313

| Fig. 314 | Fig. 315 |

small, so the left forearm is moved outward with the stretch of "Ward Off Slantingly Upward", which is different from the big angle of turning body and the oblique hitting with the open strength in Form 22. Therefore, in performing the movements of the two forms, keep in mind the difference in the main idea and in the movement of limbs.

Form 60   Grasp the Bird's Tail

(1) While shifting weight backward, turn right foot inward. Left hand is turned slightly inward, with palm facing obliquely inward; right arm is bent inward, with palm facing slightly downward. (Fig. 315)

(2) After shifting weight gradually on to right leg, sit firmly on it and change left leg into empty stance. Both arms are closed on the right side, with palms facing each other. (Fig. 316 (1), 316 (2))

Apart from the above-mentioned movements, the other movements are the same as those in Form 3. (Figs. 317, 318, 319, 320, 321, 322, 323, 324. 325, 326, 327, 328)

Points to remember:

The points are the same as those in Form 3.

Fig. 316 (1)

Fig. 316 (2)

Fig. 317

Fig. 318

Fig. 319

Fig. 320

Fig. 321

Fig. 322

Fig. 323

Fig. 324

Fig. 325

Fig. 326

Fig. 327   Fig. 328

Form 61   Single Whip

The movements and points to remember are the same as those in Form 4. (Figs. 329, 330, 331, 332, 333, 334, 335, 336)

Form 62   Fair Lady Works at Shuttles

Fair Lady Works at Shuttles (1):

(1) Shift weight backward and, with the waist leading, **turn left foot** inward (135 degrees). Left arm is bent inward, with palm **facing inward** (Fig. 337)

(2) While turning body from left to right, shift weight gradually on to left leg and change right foot into an empty step. At the same time, left arm is gradually placed below right arm; right arm is turned slightly upward, with palm facing obliquely upward. (Fig. 338)

(3) Keep right foot in the former position and turn its toes outward (45 degrees). Then, while turning body from left to right, shift weight gradually on to right foot, change left foot into an empty step and gradually raised it off the floor. At the same time, turn both arms. Left arm moves

Fig. 329   Fig. 330

Fig. 331   Fig. 332

Fig. 333

Fig. 334

Fig. 335

Fig. 336

Fig. 337

Fig. 338

along lower side of right arm and turns from below upward and from inside outward; bend right arm, with palm erect. (Figs. 339-340)

(4) Left foot comes down on floor, and both arms continue to turn. (Fig. 341)

(5) Gradually bend left leg forward to form a left bow step. Left arm is turned outward and is bent to the upper part of the left forehead, with palm facing obliquely outward; stretch right palm straight forward. Face is turned towards the southwest, with eyes looking ahead. (Fig. 342)

Fair Lady Works at Shuttles (2):

(6) Shift weight backward and, with the waist leading turn left foot inward (135 degrees) and turn the upper part of body (180 degrees). Both arms are placed downward levelly; right arm is bent to the front of abdomen and left arm is placed on the left side. (Figs. 343-344)

(7) While shifting weight gradually on to left leg, change right foot into an empty step, and turn body gradually from the left to the right rear side. At the same time, continue to move both arms in arcs from left to right. (Fig. 345)

(8) After sitting firmly on left leg, raise right foot immediately and stretch it in the southeast direction, with heel coming down on floor first.

170

Fig. 339

Fig. 341

Fig. 340

Fig. 342

171

Fig. 343

Fig. 344

Fig. 345

Continue to turn body from left to right and turn both arms; the right arm is placed below the left arm, with palm facing obliquely upward; turn left arm slightly upward, with palm facing obliquely inward. (Fig. 346)

(9) Continue to turn body from left to right, turn left foot inward and bend right leg forward to form a right bow step. Right hand is gradually turned from below upward and from inside outward, so as to gradually bend right arm to the place over the right side of the forehead, with palm facing obliquely outward. With palm erect, stretch left arm forward, with palm facing obliquely forward. Face is turned towards the southeast, and eyes look forward. (Figs. 347-348)

Fair Lady Works at Shuttles (3):

(10) Shift weight backward. At the same time, left arm is drawn back, with the left hand placed in front of the left part of abdomen; right arm is turned a little inward, with palm facing obliquely downward. (Fig. 349)

(11) While turning right foot inward, shift weight gradually on to right leg and change left foot into an empty stance. Left arm is gradually turned inward, with palm facing obliquely upward; then left arm is gradually turned from rear to front until it is below right arm, with palm facing obliquely

Fig. 346

Fig. 347   Fig. 348

Fig. 349

upward; right arm is gradually turned inward, with palm facing obliquely upward, too. (Fig. 350)

(12) Raise left foot and take a step straight forward, with heel coming down on floor first and toes raised. Left arm is turned from below upward and from inside outward; sink right elbow, with palm gradually erect. (Fig. 351)

Fig. 350   Fig. 351

(13) Bend left leg to form a left bow step. Left arm is turned outward and is bent to the upper part of the left forehead; stretch right arm forward, with palm facing obliquely outward. Face is turned toward the northeast, and eyes look forward. (Figs 352-353)

Fair Lady Works at Shuttles (4):

(14) Shift weight backward and, with the waist leading, turn left foot inward (135 degrees). Both arms are placed downward levelly at the same time. Bend right arm to the place in front of abdomen and place left arm on the left side. (Figs. 354-355)

(15) Shift weight graduallly on to left leg, change right foot into an empty stance, and turn body gradually from left to right and then to the right rear side. At the same time, continue to move both arms in an arc to the right side. (Fig. 356)

Fig. 352

Fig. 353

Fig. 354

Fig. 355

| Fig. 356 | Fig. 357 |

(16) Sit firmly on left leg and raise right foot and stretch it towards the northwest, with heel coming down on floor first. Continue to turn body from left to right and turn both arms. Right arm is placed below the left arm, with palm facing obliquely upward; left arm is turned slightly upward, with palm facing obliquely inward. (Fig. 357)

(17) Continue to turn body from left to right, bend right leg to form a right bow step. Right hand is gradually turned from below upward and from inside outward, so that the right arm is gradually bent to the right upper part of the forehead, with palm facing obliquely outward. With the palm erect, the left arm is stretched forward, with palm facing obliquely forward. Face is turned towards the northwest, with eyes looking ahead. (Figs. 358-359)

Points to remember:

(1) There are four styles in this form — in four oblique angles, as shown in the illustrations.

(2) Because the range of turning the body is relatively great, the movement of raising leg and stepping forward is not completed all at once. In Style (1) and Style (3), there is a transition between raising the leg and stepping forward. In Style (2) and Style (4), the range is much greater; though

Fig. 358   Fig. 359

there is no transition between raising the leg and stepping forward, the movement of turning foot inward after turning the body should be done in two parts, that is, turn foot inward twice. The first time the body is turned, it is 180 degrees, and the foot is turned 135 degrees; the second time, both body and foot are turned 90 degrees. Thus, the body is turned 270 degrees and foot 225 degrees in all.

(3) Whenever turning the body in a great angle, the importance of using the waist to lead and coordinate the movement of the four limbs becomes more conspicuous. Failing to do so, the upper and lower limbs will not be able to move in coordination and there will be no continuity in the movements, and the body will not be able to maintain an upright position.

(4) All lower arms, which are turned from below upward and from inside outward until they are bent to the upper part of the forehead, should push the opposing party upward with the strength of "Ward Off Slantingly Upward". The palm which stretches forward is also for the purpose of hitting the chest of the opposing party.

Form 63   Grasp the Bird's Tail

(1) While shifting weight backward, right arm is bent from above

178

downward and is stretched levelly, with palm facing obliquely downward; left arm is turned inward, with palm facing obliquely inward, and is placed below right elbow to form the pulling stance. (Fig. 360)

Fig. 360

(2) Turn right foot inward (90 degrees), with toes pointing to the southwest; shift weight on to right leg and bend left leg naturally into an empty step in its original place. At the same time, right arm is bent from below outward, upward and then inward; right palm is placed between chest and abdomen, with palm facing downward. Left arm is turned and then bent inward, with palm facing obliquely upward, and is placed in front of abdomen. Both arms are closed. After sitting firmly on right leg, left leg is immediately stretched straight forward, with heel coming down on floor first and toes raised slightly.

The remaining movements are basically the same as those in Form 3, with only a slight difference in the connecting movements. The points to remember are the same, too. (Figs. 361, 362, 363, 364, 365, 366, 367, 368, 369, 370, 371, 372, 373, 374)

Form 64   Single Whip

The movements and points to remember are the same as those in Form 4. (Figs. 375, 376, 377, 378, 379, 380, 381, 382)

Fig. 361

Fig. 362

Fig. 363

Fig. 364

Fig. 365

Fig. 366

Fig. 367

Fig. 368

Fig. 369

Fig. 370

Fig. 371

Fig. 372

Fig. 373

Fig. 374

Fig. 375

Fig. 376

Fig. 377

Fig. 378

Fig. 379

Fig. 380

Fig. 381

Fig. 382

Form 65　　Wave Hands Like
Clouds on Both Sides (1)

The movements and points to remember are the same as those in Form 32. (Figs. 383, 384, 385, 386, 387, 388, 389, 390)

Form 66　　Wave Hands Like
Clouds on Both Sides (2)

The movement and points to remember are the same as those in Form 33. (Figs. 391, 392, 393, 394, 395, 396)

Form 67　　Wave Hands Like
Clouds on Both Sides (3)

The movements and points to remember are the same as those in Form 34. (Figs. 397, 398, 399)

Form 68　　Single Whip

The movements and points to remember are the same as those in Form 35. (Figs. 400, 401, 402)

Fig. 383

Fig. 384

Fig. 385   Fig. 386

Fig. 387   Fig. 388

Fig. 389

Fig. 390

Fig. 391

Fig. 392

Fig. 393

Fig. 394

Fig. 395

Fig. 396

Fig. 397

Fig. 398

Fig. 399

Fig. 400

Fig. 401

Fig. 402

Form 69   Push Down

Turn right foot outward (90 degrees) and, in the direction of the toes, turn body to the right, bend right leg and squat down. Then, gradually shift weight on to right leg and stretch left leg leftward. At the same time, following the shifting of weight, left palm is withdrawn gradually from front to rear, past the chest, until it is in front of abdomen, with the palm facing obliquely rightward and fingers pointing to the front. Face is turned to the southeast, and eyes look at the lower right side to the front. (Fig. 403)

Fig. 403

Points to remember:

(1) In this form, the posture is low and it is necessary to bend the leg and squat down. Therefore, you should guard against inclining the upper part of the body forward and don't stick out the hips. In other words, keep the upper part of the body erect.

(2) The rear foot (right foot) must be turned outward (90 degrees), otherwise you will not be able to bend right leg and squat down.

(3) Left arm is moved along with the shifting of weight from front to rear in an arc past the chest and is placed in front of abdomen on the inner side of left leg. The arc should not be too big.

(4) If you cannot squat down, the posture may be a bit higher. But you should always guard against drooping the head, bending the waist and sticking up the hips.

Form 70   Golden Cock Stands on
One Leg (Right Style)

(1) Move the four limbs along with the waist. First turn right foot inward (90 degrees, turn to its former place) and then turn left foot outward (45 degrees). Following the movement of waist, shift weight gradually on to left leg. (Figs. 404-405)

Fig. 404   Fig. 405

(2) Continue to shift weight on to left leg and raise right foot gradually off the floor. Change right hooked hand into palm and move it from rear in a forward and downward arc to the place beside the right hip; press left arm down from front to rear. (Fig. 406)

(3) While raising the upper part of body, straighten the left leg; raise right leg and bend shank, with toes pointing a little downward. Bend right elbow with palm erect and facing the left side and fingers pointing upward. Continue to press left arm downward until it is beside the left hip, with

palm facing downward and fingers pointing to the front. Face is turned due east, with eyes looking straight ahead. (Fig. 407)

Fig. 406   Fig. 407

Form 71   Golden Cook Stands on
One Leg (Left Style)

(1) Left leg is bent and right leg falls on floor. Then, draw right foot half a step backward, with toes coming down first on floor in the direction of 45 degrees, then sit firmly on right foot and change left foot into an empty stance, with toes raised. While turning body slightly to the right, bend left elbow, with palm erect, and raise arm; move right hand from above in a downward arc and press it down.(Figs. 408-409)

(2) Stand straight on right leg; raise left leg and bend its shank downward, with toes pointing slightly downward. Continue to raise left arm, with palm facing the right side and fingers pointing upward. Press right hand downward until it is beside the right hip, with palm facing downward and fingers pointing to the front. Face is turned due east, and eyes look straight ahead. (Fig. 410)

Points to remember:

(1) After turning right foot inward, and left foot outward, and gra-

Fig. 408

Fig. 409

Fig. 410

dually shifting weight forward, both feet still have the strength of straightening and kicking out and the sustaining strength, so that the right leg and the two arms have the meaning of movement of the next action.

(2) The turning of one foot inward and the other outward has a bearing on the correct posture and at the same time facilitates the next movement. If you don't turn the right foot inward, you cannot stand up, and if you don't turn the left foot outward, your body will be inclined. So you should pay special attention to this action when standing up after shifting the weight forward.

(3) The first form in "Golden Cock Stands on One Leg" is the right style, that is, use right leg to attack the other party. This is the same as kicking towards the right side in "Separation of Right Foot" (Form 37). The next form is the left style, which has the same meaning as the former, the only difference is using the left leg instead of the right leg.

(4) In this form, the low posture is directly changed to high posture, which is different from the actions in the medium posture and also different from the actions of changing from the medium posture to the high posture. Because of the larger amount of action, it is difficult for you to control the movements, so it is necessary to pay attention to the coordination of movement of the whole body. You should use the waist to lead the movement of the four limbs and carefully coordinate their movements. Only in this way will the upper and lower limbs move in unison and in a smooth and round manner.

Form 72   Step Back and Repulse the Monkey (Right Style)

(1) Turn both arms. Left arm is stretched forward, with palm turned upward; right arm is turned inward, with palm turned upward, and then it is moved in a downward arc to the right rear at the shoulder level. (Fig. 411)

(2) Right leg is bent a bit and left leg falls on floor. Then, left foot is stretched backward half a step, with toes coming down first on floor in the direction of 45 degrees. At the same time, right arm is bent upward with its palm erect and facing obliquely forward. (Fig. 412)

(3) With the waist leading, shift weight gradually on to left leg and sit firmly on it. Change right leg into empty stance and at the same time turn right foot inward and place it in the front. Continue to withdraw left arm to the side of left hip to form an arc, with palm facing upward; continue to

Fig. 411

Fig. 412

stretch right arm forward, with palm facing forward. Face is turned due east; body is inclined to the left side (45 degrees) with eyes looking ahead. (Fig. 413)

Form 73   Step Back and Repulse the Monkey (Left Style)

The movements and points to remember are the same as those in Form 20. (Figs. 414, 415, 416, 417, 418, 419)

Form 74   Step Back and Repulse the Monkey (Right Style)

The movements and points to remember are the same as those in Form 21. (Figs 420, 421, 422, 423)

Form 75   Slant Flying

The movements and points to remember are the same as those in Form 22. (Figs. 424, 425, 426, 427)

Fig. 413

Fig. 414

Fig. 415

Fig. 416

Fig. 417

Fig. 418

Fig. 419

Fig. 420

Fig. 421

Fig. 422

Fig. 423

Fig. 424

Fig. 425

Fig. 426

Fig. 427

Form 76   Raise Hands and Step Up

The movements and points to remember are the same as those in From 23. (Figs. 428, 429, 430, 431, 432, 433, 434, 435)

Form 77   White Crane Spreads Its Wings

The movements and points to remember are the same as those in Form 24. (Figs 436-437. Fig. 438 being the front view)

Form 78   Brush Knee and Twist Step (Left Style)

The movements and points to remember are the same as those in Form 25. (Figs. 439, 440, 441, 442, 443)

Form 79   Needle at Sea Bottom

The movements and points to remember are the same as those in Form 26. (Figs. 444, 445, 446)

Fig. 428

Fig. 429

Fig. 430

Fig. 431

Fig. 432

Fig. 433

Fig. 434

Fig. 435

Fig. 436

Fig. 437

Fig. 438

Fig. 439

Fig. 440

Fig. 441

Fig. 442

Fig. 443

Fig. 444

Fig. 445

Fig. 446

Form 80   Fan Through the Back

The movements and points to remember are the same as those in Form 27. (Figs. 447-448)

Fig. 447   Fig 448

Form 81   White Snake Puts
Out Its Tongue

(1) Shift weight backward and, with the waist leading, turn body from the left to the right rear and turn left foot inward (135 degrees). In the course of turning the left foot, gradually shift weight on to left leg and sit firmly on it, then change right foot into an empty stance. Left arm is bent inward and left hand is placed over the left forehead, with palm facing outward; right arm is moved from above in a downward arc to the place between chest and abdomen, with palm facing downward. (Figs 449, 450, 451)

(2) Move the four limbs along with the waist. Continue to turn body from left to right, raise right foot and stretch it straight forward to land on the floor (180 degrees, from due east to due west). At the same time, left arm comes to the side of left rib, with the palm erect and facing obliquely

Fig. 449

Fig. 450

Fig. 451

forward; right arm is turned upward and forward to enable the back of the hand stretch forward and downward, with palm facing obliquely upward. (Fig. 452)

(3) Shift weight to the right to form a right bow step. At the same time, right arm is moved from the front in a downward arc and withdrawn to the side of right hip, with palm facing upward; left arm is stretched forward with palm facing the front. Face is turned due west, and eyes look ahead. (Fig. 453)

Fig. 452   Fig. 453

Points to remember:

(1) In this form, there are many complex and continuous movements. Therefore, pay attention to the coordination and continuity of movements, and the transition actions among them should not be regarded as fixed forms.

(2) In the course of turning the body, the angle of turning foot inward should be 135 degrees. If the angle is not large enough, it will be difficult to stretch right leg out. This is also so with the upper part of the body. Therefore, the angle of turning the foot plays an important stabilizing role in keeping the body erect and coordinating the movements of other parts. So long as the base is firm, you can move nimbly and turn in a mooth and round manner.

Form 82   Step Up, Deflect Downward, Parry and Punch

(1) Shift weight leftward, change right foot into an empty step and turn body from right to left. Right arm is bent and right palm follows the waist and move gradually inward and forward to the left oblique angle, with palm facing obliquely downward; left arm is bent inward to the left lower side of right arm, with elbow sunk and facing obliquely upward. At the same time, with the waist leading the movement of arm, clench right fist gradually, sink wrist and move fist to the left side. (Figs. 454-455 being the front view. Figs. 456, 457, 458)

Fig. 454

Fig. 455

(2) While shifting weight gradually rightward, left foot is gradually raised from the floor. Following the waist, both arms are moved upward in arcs. Along with the shifting of weight, the back of right fist is moved from the left to the right side, with the back of fist stretched tight and clenched fingers facing obliquely inward. Left arm follows the right fist, its palm erect and ready to stretch forward. (Fig. 459)

(3) Raise left leg and stretch it straight forward, with heel coming down on floor and toes raised. Left palm is stretched forward, and right

Fig. 456

Fig. 457

Fig. 458

fist is drawn back to the place near the side of right hip to form an arc, with clenched fingers facing upward. (Fig. 460)

Fig. 459

Fig. 460

(4) Shift weight gradually on to left leg, bend left leg to form a left bow step. Right arm is turned inward, with the knuckles of fist facing the front, and then it is stretched forward; meanwhile, left hand is withdrawn from the front to the place near the right rib, with fingers pointing upward, palm facing rightward and both arms shoulder-width apart. Face is turned due west and eyes look straight ahead. (Fig. 461)

Points to remember:

(1) This form is a continuous action of Form 81, but it is somewhat different from Form 29 which is a continuous action of Form 28. The difference lies in the transition action. In Form 29, right arm is moved with its fist, while in this form, it is moved with its palm. Please see the front views in both forms for reference.

(2) The other points are the same as those in Form 29.

Form 83 Step Up and Grasp the Bird's Tail

The movements and points to remember are the same as those in Form 30. (Figs. 462, 463, 464, 465, 466, 467, 468, 469, 470, 471, 472)

Fig. 461

Fig. 462

Fig. 463

214

Fig. 464

Fig. 465

Fig. 466

Fig. 467

Fig. 468

Fig. 469

Fig. 470

Fig. 471

Fig. 472

Form 84   Single Whip

The movements and points to remember are the same as those in Form 4. (Figs. 473, 474, 475, 476, 477, 478, 479)

Form 85   Wave Hands Like Clouds
on Both Sides (1)

The movements and points to remember are the same as those in Form 32. (Figs. 480, 481, 482, 483, 484, 485, 486, 487)

Form 86   Wave Hands Like Clouds
on Both Sides (2)

The movements and points to remember are the same as those in Form 33. (Figs. 488, 489, 490, 491, 492, 493)

Form 87   Wave Hands Like Clouds
on Both Sides (3)

The movements and points to remember are the same as those in Form 34. (Figs. 494, 495, 496)

Fig. 473

Fig. 474

Fig. 475

Fig. 476

Fig. 477

Fig. 478

Fig. 479

Fig. 480

Fig. 481

Fig. 482

Fig. 483

Fig. 484   Fig. 485

Fig. 486

Fig. 487

Fig. 488

Fig. 489

Fig. 490

Fig. 491

Fig. 492

Fig. 493

Fig. 494

Fig. 495

Fig. 496

Form 88　　Single Whip

The movements and points to remember are the same as those in Form 35. (Figs. 497, 498, 499)

Form 89　　High Pat on Horse and
Go with Palm

(1) This movement is the same as the one in Form 36. (Figs. 500, 501, 502)

(2) Raise left foot and sit firmly on right leg. Stretch left leg forward with heel coming down on floor first. Then, gradually shift weight on to left leg and bend it to form a left bow step. While turning body from left to right, right arm is gradually bent from front to rear and then inward until it is below left armpit, with palm facing downward; left arm is moved from rear to front, with palm facing upward. Face is turned due east; body is turned to the southeast, with eyes looking straight ahead. (Figs. 503-504)

Points to remember:

(1) The first movement and the points to remember are the same as those in Form 36.

Fig. 497

Fig. 498

Fig. 499

Fig. 500

Fig. 501

Fig. 502

Fig. 503   Fig. 504

(2) When you stretch left leg out, the heel must come down on floor first so that you can straighten the rear leg, sustain with the front leg and shift weight gradually forward. You should not let toes come down on floor first, because if you do so, the upper part of your body is likely to incline, the hips will stick out, both arms will lose their coordination and you will not be able to really perform the action of raising your left hand from rear to front to hit the opponent's throat.

Form 90   Cross Legs

(1) While shifting weight backward, turn left foot inward (135 degrees) and turn body from left to right. (Fig. 505)

(2) Gradually shift weight on to left leg and change right foot into an empty step. Right arm is turned from the place below left armpit, with palm facing inward, to form an oblique cross with left arm. (Fig. 506)

(3) Stand up on left leg, raise right leg and kick forward with its heel. Arms are separated and moved to both sides at the same time. Face is turned due west; body is turned to the southwest, with eyes looking straight ahead. (Figs. 507-508)

Fig. 505

Fig. 506

Fig. 507

Fig. 508

Points to remember:

(1) The movements in this form are similar to those in Form 51, but there is a little difference in usage. In this form, while turning the body, the left palm has the meaning of attacking the opponent's chest, which is different from that in Form 51.

(2) For the other points, you may refer to those in Form 51.

Form 91   Step Up and Punch Opponent's Pubic Region

(1) Left leg is bent and right one falls with heel coming down on floor. Turn right foot outward (45 degrees) and turn body from left to right. Then, shift weight gradually on to right leg and raise left foot off the floor. At the same time, right arm is bent inward and its palm is changed into fist, with the clenched fingers facing obliquely upward and placed in front of right hip; left arm is bent a little inward, with palm facing obliquely downward and placed in front of abdomen. (Fig. 509)

(2) Raise left foot and stretch it straight forward, with heel coming down on floor first. (Fig. 510)

(3) Move the four limbs along with the waist. Turn body from right to left, bend waist and incline the upper part of body slightly forward. Shift

Fig. 509

Fig. 510

weight gradually on to left leg and bend it to form a left bow step. At the same time, both arms are moved from rear to front. Left hand is moved in an arc, past the knee, to the side of left knee, with palm facing downward and fingers pointing forward; right fist is turned with the knuckles facing the front to hit the opponent's crotch. Body is turned due west, and eyes look at the opponent's crotch. (Fig. 511)

Fig. 511

Form 92   Step Up and Grasp
the Bird's Tail

The movements and points to remember are the same as those in Form 30. (Figs. 512, 513, 514, 515, 516, 517, 518, 519, 520, 521, 522)

Form 93   Single Whip

The movements and points to remember are the same as those in Form 4. (Figs 523, 524, 525, 526, 527, 528, 529, 530)

Form 94   Push Down

The movements and points to remember are the same as those in Form 69. (Fig. 531)

230

Fig. 512

Fig. 513

Fig. 514

Fig. 515

Fig. 516

Fig. 517

Fig. 518

Fig. 519

Fig. 520

Fig. 521

Fig. 522

Fig. 523

Fig. 524

Fig. 525

Fig. 526

Fig. 527

Fig. 528

Fig. 529

Fig. 530

Fig. 531

Form 95   Step Up to Form Seven Stars

(1) Move the four limbs along with the waist. Turn right foot inward (90 degrees, to the former place) and left foot outward (45 degrees). Shift weight gradually on to left leg. (Fig. 532)

Fig. 532

(2) Continue to shift weight on to left leg and raise right foot gradually off the floor. Right hooked hand is loosened and makes as if it is going to clench the fist; then it moves in a downward arc from rear to front until it comes to the side of right hip; left arm is bent a little inward. (Fig. 533)

(3) Continue to shift weight forward on to left leg, turn body leftward and straighten up slowly. After sitting firmly on left leg, raise right leg and stretch it forward, with toes coming down on floor to form a right empty step. At the same time, clench both fists; left fist is bent to the place in front of chest and right fist is bent from below upward to the place under the left fist, with the two fists now crossed at the shoulder level. Face is turned due east, with eyes looking straight ahead. (Fig. 534)

Points to remember:

(1) The points to remember in the first and second movements are the

Fig. 533   Fig. 534

same as those in Form 69.

(2) While body is raised slowly, the clenched right fist has the meaning of hitting out, and it is not placed idly under the left fist. Both arms should also have the meaning of hitting out. Pay attention to the right empty step so as to avoid sticking out the hips or shrugging the shoulders.

(3) When crossing the arms in front of chest, be sure that they don't touch the body.

(4) The fists face obliquely downward, which has the meaning of punching the opponent with both fists.

Form 96   Retreat to Ride the Tiger

(1) Raise right leg and take a step backward; shift weight backward, turn body slightly to the right and change left foot into empty stance. At the same time, following body, right arm is drawn back to the place in front of right hip; left hand is changed into fist to form a hitting posture. (Fig. 535)

(2) Sit firmly on right leg and form left foot into an empty step. Both fists are changed into palms at the same time. Right arm is bent from below outward and then upward until it is above the right side of the forehead, with palm facing outward and fingers pointing leftward; left arm is

moved from front-backward to the side of left hip. Face is turned due east, with eyes looking straight ahead. (Fig. 536)

Fig. 535

Fig. 536

Points to remember:

(1) In this form, while stepping back, right foot should not be placed on the same straight line as the left foot, otherwise you will lose your balance. But if you should take too big a step to the right as you step backward, it will also affect the correct posture. So this step should be taken in an appropriate way.

(2) While stepping back, you should not move the hips first, but should use the waist to lead the four limbs to move backward. That is to say, you should keep your head erect as if there were something on it, sink your breath into abdomen, keep the waist and hips relaxed, and keep the chest and back in their natural position. You should have a clear idea of these actions and coordinate them well. Though you step backward, there is the implied meaning of going forward.

(3) While separating the two arms upward and downward, don't move them in too big an arc, otherwise the movements will not be tightly knit.

Form 97   Turn Round and Kick Horizontally

(1) Move both arms in arcs. Right arm is moved in a rightward and downward arc to the place below left arm, with palm facing downward and fingers pointing leftward; left arm is moved in a leftward and upward arc and is slightly bent and placed in the front, with palm facing downward and fingers pointing to the front right side. (Figs. 537-538)

Fig. 537   Fig. 538

(2) Move the four limbs along with the waist. With the left toes as the axis, turn body from left to right (180 degrees). At the same time, right arm is moved in a big arc from inside outward; left arm is gradually bent from the front inward until it is between the chest and abdomen. (Fig. 539)

(3) After sitting firmly on right leg, raise left foot and stretch it as you continue to turn body (225 degrees) in the southeast direction. (Figs. 540, 541, 542)

(4) After shifting weight on to left leg, stand up and raise right leg, with toes pointing slightly downward. Right arm is in front and left arm is behind, with both palms facing downward. (Fig. 543)

(5) With the waist leading, right foot is moved in a rightward and up-

Fig. 539

Fig. 540

Fig. 541

Fig. 542   Fig. 543

ward arc, with instep moving outward. At the same time, move both palms
from right to left towards right foot to pat its instep (left palm first and
right palm following it). After patting, stand firm on left leg and bend right
leg, with toes pointing downward; both arms are placed on the left side to
form the pulling posture, with both palms facing downward. Face is turned
towards the southeast, with eyes looking straight ahead. (Figs. 544, 545,
546, 547)

Points to remember:

(1) In this form, turn body from left to right for 405 degrees in all,
that is, from due east, turn round and then let foot fall in the southeast direction. The range is greater than that in Form 51 (360 degrees), so you
must keep a proper balance. To make the turning smooth and round, in ad-
dition to taking the right toes as the axis, it is necessary to use the waist to
coordinate the movements of the upper and lower part of the body, otherwise the lower part of body will not be stable and the upper part will move
from side to side. Of course, the body should not be stiff, but should relax
so as to coordinate all parts to successfully complete the big turn.

(2) The action of moving foot horizontally and pat instep with palms
should vary from person to person. If you cannot pat the instep, don't over-

Fig. 544

Fig. 545

Fig. 546

Fig. 547

strain yourself to do it, othrwise your limbs will fall into disarray and you may cut a grotesque figure. In short, you should do this action naturally and as far as you can manage it.

(3) Because the right foot is used to kick horizontally at the chest and ribs of the opponent, it should not be raised too high.

Form 98   Shoot the Tiger with Bow

(1) Left leg is bent and right leg falls with heel coming down on floor and toes raised. (Figs 548)

Fig. 548

(2) Move the four limbs along with the waist, turn body from left to right, straighten the left leg and sustain with right leg; shift weight gradually forward. Following the waist, both arms are moved in a downward arc, past the knee, until they come to the right side; meanwhile, both hands are gradually changed into fists. (Figs. 549-550)

(3) Shift weight on to right leg to form a right bow step. At the same time, following the waist, both arms hit from the right to the left front. Right fist is placed in front of right side of the forehead, with the part between thumb and index finger facing obliquely downward; left fist is placed in front of the left part of chest, with the part between thumb and in-

Fig. 549   Fig. 550

dex finger facing obliquely upward and clenched fingers facing obliquely
outward. Face is turned to the northeast, and eyes look straight ahead
(Fig. 551)

Points to remember:

(1) When right foot comes down on floor, turn body gradually from
left to right and bend leg gradually forward; this should be in keeping with
the action of moving both arms from left to right and then from right to
left with body turned to hit at the opponent. Because the movement of the
arms covers a much greater range than the bending of leg, the speed of
moving the lower limbs should therefore be well controlled, otherwise the
legs will not move in unison with the arms.

(2) Because the two arms hit out in a different direction from that of
the bending of leg, you should therefore guard against inclining the upper
part of body while turning the body leftward and stretching out the arms.

Form 99   Step Up, Deflect
Downward, Parry and Punch

(1) While turning left toes outward to the northeast, turn right toes
inward. Shift weight gradually on to left leg and from the posture of deflect-

Fig. 551

ing downward. The other movements are the same as those in Form 14. (Figs. 552, 553, 554, 555. 556, 557)

Points to remember:

The points are the same as those in Form 14.

Form 100   Apparent Close-Up

The movements and points to remember are the same as those in Form 15. (Figs. 558, 559, 560, 561)

Form 101   Crose Hands

The movements and points to remember are the same as those in Form 16. (Figs. 562, 563, 564, 565, 566)

Form 102   Closing Form

Stand straight on both legs. Move the two arms in different directions to both sides, shoulder-width apart; then gradually move them in downward arcs until they are in front of the hips, with palms facing downward and fingers pointing to the front. Face is turned due south, with eyes looking straight ahead. (Figs. 567, 568, 569)

Fig. 552

Fig. 553

Fig. 554

Fig. 555

Fig. 556   Fig. 557

Fig. 558   Fig. 559

247

Fig. 560

Fig. 561

Fig. 562

Fig. 563

Fig. 564

Fig. 565

Fig. 566

Fig. 567

Fig. 568

Fig. 569

Points to remember:

This form is the same as the commencing form. It is the end of the whole series, and it is often neglected, which is of course wrong. Practising *Taijiquan* helps cultivate one's character and good habit of doing things in a thorough manner from beginning to end. Moreover, though this is the closing form, there is still the meaning of movement in it, and that is why many people repeat it several times before the end.

Form 103   Restoring Form

In this form you return to the normal position. (Fig. 570)

Fig. 570

HOW TO USE *TAIJIQUAN*

(With Illustrations)

Yang Zhenduo

The methods of application of *Taijiquan* given here are compiled on the basis of "Taijiquan, its Applications and Variations", a posthumous work by Yang Chengfu, my late father. In it there is a portrait of my father together with 37 photographs, each of which gives a lively and clear picture of the movements. In particular, they demonstrate the spirit, essence and typical style of *Taijiquan* in all their richness. The movements are dignified, natural and unrestrained, showing the high level of attainment. The photographs are really precious, and I had the intention of reprinting and enclosing them here for the benefit of all who love *Taijiquan*. Unfortunately, the plates have become blurred over the years, and to make up for this irreparable loss, I have tried to imitate the movements in the original photographs and had some photographs taken, which are printed in this book. My skill, however, is limited, and the best I can do is to imitate the postures, but I cannot bring out the spirit. Nevertheless, it is my hope that these photographs will be of help to all who wish to learn *Taijiquan*.

In the book "*Taijiquan*, Its Applications and Variations", explanations were given to practically all the forms, together with examples and illustrations. But some forms were not fully explained. For example, in the form "Grasp the Bird's Tail", there are the movements of "Ward Off Slantingly Upward", "Pull Back", "Press Forward" and "Push", but only the "Push" movement is explained with illustrations. Thus learners cannot get a picture of the applications of this form. In order to help learners get a complete idea, I shall explain with illustrations the movements in "Single Whip", "Deflect Downward, Parry and Punch" and "Apparent Close-Up". Because the methods of application given here are all based on suppositions, they can only serve as examples to arouse the interest of the trainees in practice. Of course, they can be of help to those who wish to further improve their techniques in *Taijiquan*. However, these examples cannot be applied or copied mechanically. When you learn and practise *Taijiquan*, what you really do is to learn and practise the Thirteen Poses of *Taiji* (Ward Off Slantingly Upward, Pull Back, Press Forward, Push, Pull Down, Bend Backward, Elbow-Stroke, Shoulder-Stroke, Advance, Retreat, Look to the Left, Look to the Right, Central Equilibrium), that is, learn and practise the co-ordination of the hands, eyes, body and steps. The applications, however, vary very much under different circumstances, so it is necessary to take advantage of every opportunity and act according to circumstances so as to transform adversity into advantage. In short, you should apply the skills according to the actual conditions. Whether a trainee can apply the techniques well or not depends on himself, I can therefore only give some idea of the methods of application and not deal with them in detail.

To enable the trainees understand the applications of the various forms more clearly and in a realistic way, I have chosen the method of pitting two persons against each other and explain the movements with the help of illustrations. As the movements are based on suppositions, I shall explain with illustrations the meaning of the movements one by one in their sequence according to my own understanding. This inevitably has its limitations as far as the concrete actions and methods of application are concerned, and it will be difficult to fully bring out the flexibility of the Thirteen Poses of Taiji. Though the applications of each form are changeable and have a certain association with speed, they cannot be too far divorced from fixed pose of each form. Therefore, in order not to let the learners feel at a loss as to what to do, I only deal with the forms and I will not take up too many variations or give more examples of methods to meet emergency.

Methods of application: There are altogether 92 illustrations, which explain the movements one by one according to the sequence of the Series of Taijiquan. Repetitious actions appear only once, and as regards some forms in which there are both left and right styles, explanations are given only to one side; but in the more complicated forms, explanations with illustrations are given to both sides.

In "Grasp the Bird's Tail", there are the four methods of "Ward Off Slantingly Upward", "Pull Back", "Press Forward" and "Push". They are the main sources of the variations of the hand skill in *Taijiquan* and play a very important role. That is why special emphasis is placed on the requirement that "warding off, pulling back, pressing forward and pushing must be done conscientiously" in the Song of Pushing Hands. Therefore, whether in giving examples or in explaining, I have dealt with them in greater detail. Moreover, I have given explanations on the actions of emitting strength in "Pull Back", "Press Forward" and "Push" for the benefit of the learners. I hope that trainees will learn them conscientiously so as to lay a good foundation for learning "Push Hands" later on.

In order to be concise, I have tried to make the explanations short and easily understood. Some transition actions in application are not mentioned or explained in detail, but trainees may look them up in the Series for reference. Some actions are not completely identical with those in the Series. For example, in the fixed pose of "Brush Knee and Twist Step (Left Style)", the left hand is placed beside the left knee with the fingers pointing forward; but in the illustration on the method of application for the same form, the left hand is used to hold the opponent's right wrist. Though the actions of the left hand seem to be different in the two cases, they are really the same in application. That is to say, when my left arm is moved from above downward with body turned leftward, in that very instant it touches the opponent with the hand skill of "Pull Down", but the point of contact depends on the height and speed of the opponent's action. The upper arm, elbow, forearm, wrist or hand are all possible points of contact. My purpose is to keep clear of the opponent's hand which is trying to hit me and to convert an adverse position into an advantageous one so as to subdue the opponent. As to the height or shape of my hand, it should not be restricted by the fixed pose in the Series. You should understand and apply the method dialectically, not mechanically.

In the illustrations, the man dressed in white represents "I" in the explanations, while the man dressed in black represents the "opponent".

NAMES OF THE FORMS OF APPLICATION OF THE YANG SCHOOL OF *TAIJIQUAN*

Yang Zhenduo

Form   1   Grasp the Bird's Tail
Form   2   Single Whip
Form   3   Raise Hands and Step Up
Form   4   White Crane Spreads Its Wings
Form   5   Brush Knee and Twist Step (Left Style)
Form   6   Hand Strums the Lute
Form   7   Deflect Downward, Parry and Punch
Form   8   Apparent Close-Up
Form   9   Cross Hands
Form   10   Carry the Tiger to the Mountain
Form   11   Fist Under Elbow
Form   12   Step Back and Repulse the Monkey
Form   13   Slant Flying
Form   14   Needle at Sea Bottom
Form   15   Fan Through the Back
Form   16   Chop Opponent with Fist
Form   17   Wave Hands Like Clouds on Both Sides
Form   18   High Pat on Horse
Form   19   Separation of Right Foot
Form   20   Turn and Kick with left Heel
Form   21   Step Up and Punch Downward
Form   22   Hit the Tiger
Form   23   Strike Opponent's Ears with Both Fists
Form   24   Part the Wild Horse's Mane
Form   25   Fair Lady Works at Shuttles
Form   26   Push Down
Form   27   Golden Cock Stands on One Leg
Form   28   White Snake Puts Out Its Tongue
Form   29   High Pat on Horse and Go with Palm
Form   30   Cross Legs
Form   31   Step Up and Punch Opponent's Pubic Region

Form 1   Grasp the Bird's Tail

This form is divided into "Ward Off Slantingly Upward — Left Style (with single hand)", "Ward Off Slantingly Upward — Right Style (with both hands)", "Pull Back", "Press Forward" and "Push". Together they are called "Grasp the Bird's Tail."

Ward Off Slantingly Upward — Left Style

If the opponent hits at me with his left palm, I immediately raise my left arm to fend off his arm with the strength of "Ward Off Slantingly Upward" (sticking strength) and keep it away from my chest. And if, with the waist leading, I turn my arm and hand outward with palm turned outward, I can catch hold of the opponent's arm and divert his force to one side with the strength of "Pull Down" so as to make him miss the target and lose his balance. In this way, the opponent will be subdued by me (Fig. 1)

Ward Off Slantingly Upward — Right Style (with both hands):

Fig. 1

If the opponent hits me with his left palm, I quickly stretch my right leg forward and place my right arm below his left arm close to the elbow. At the same time, I turn my left palm obliquely outward to press the opponent's wrist, hold it and then ward off slantingly upward with my right arm; meanwhile, I use my left hand which is below to pull and press the opponent's forearm. At this time, the opponent's elbow is in a bad position because his upper arm is being pushed up while his forearm is being pressed downward. Under these circumstances, he will not be able to keep his feet and his arm may even be broken. (Figs. 2-3)

Fig. 2   Fig. 3

Pull Back:

Following the preceding form, if the opponent sinks his elbow and tries to escape when he feels that I will break his arm, I immediately turn my body from left to right, turn my right arm inward, place it on the back of his elbow, and press it downward from right to left; at the same time I lift my left hand which is holding the opponent's wrist. Thus, with my right arm pressing downward and my left hand pushing upward, the opponent's elbow is in a bad position, which naturally makes the opponent lose his balance and unable to control himself. (Figs. 4, 5, 6)

Fig. 7 shows the action of emitting force, that is, hitting the opponent with explosive force. In emitting force, be sure that the actions of the whole body are well coordinated.

Fig. 4   Fig. 5

Fig. 6

Press Forward:

Following the preceding form, if the opponent draws back his left arm when he feels that I have the intention of pressing his elbow downward, I immediately turn my right arm inward with the palm facing inward, and place my left hand on my right forearm with the palm facing outward. (Fig. 8) While the opponent draws back his arm, I quickly seize the opportunity to press forward. (Figs. 9-10) In this way, the opponent will fall backward. (Fig. 11 shows the action of emitting force.)

Fig. 7

Fig. 8

Fig. 9

Fig. 10

Push:

If the opponent is prepared before I press forward and again sinks his elbow to free himself, I immediately place my right hand on the back of his hand near the wrist with my palm facing outward, and at the same time place my left hand, also with the palm facing outward, on his elbow to control the joints of his wrist and elbow. (Figs. 12, 13, 14) Then, I push forward with both hands. Fig. 15 shows the action of emitting force.

Fig. 11

Fig. 12

Fig. 13

Form 2   Single Whip

If someone attacks me from behind or from one side. I immediately turn my body and move my arms along with the waist. At the same time, I

Fig. 14

Fig. 15

Fig. 16

Fig. 17

change my right palm into a hooked hand. When I have turned round to the place in front of the opponent's chest, I hit his chest with my wrist. (Fig. 16) If the opponent discovers this quickly enough and draws in his chest to keep clear of my wrist, I can quickly raise my right hand and hit his chin when he bends his head down. (Fig. 17).

If another person hits my back from the other side, I immediately turn my body and strike him with my left plam. (Fig. 18)

Form 3   Raise Hands and Step Up

If the opponent attacks my right side with his left palm, I immediately turn my body from left to right, and along with it turn my foot inward. Now facing my opponent, I sit firmly on my left leg and raise my right foot, stretch it forward and quickly place my right hand on the upper part of his left elbow and hold his left wrist with my left hand. At the same time, I press both hands to break his elbow with the force thus generated. Under my concerted attack with one hand forcing inward and the other outward, my opponent will lose control of himself. (Fig. 19)

If the opponent reacts quickly and draws in his chest and sinks his elbow in an attempt to escape when he discovers that his left arm will be

Fig. 18

Fig. 19

subdued, I can take the opportunity to turn my right wrist inward, with my palm turned obliquely upward, and place my left hand between the elbow and wrist, with my palm facing outward. In this way I press the opponent backward. (Figs. 20-21)

Form 4   White Crane Spreads Its Wings

If the opponent attacks me from the left side with both hands, I immediately turn my body to the left front side, with my right foot turned inward, shift weight on to right leg and sit firmly on it. Then, I change my left foot into empty stance, with the heel slightly raised and toes on the floor. At the same time, I close both hands in front of my chest, ward off the op-

262

Fig. 20

Fig. 21

ponent's right arm (or hand, or fist) with my right forearm and force it upward to the right side over his head, with my palm facing outward. I place
my left hand on the inside of my right forearm, with the palm facing downward to protect my chest and abdomen or hold the opponent's left hand
and pull it downward. Thus, by pushing one of my hands upward and sinking the other hand, I can divert the opponent's force and subdue him. (Figs.

Fig. 22

Fig. 23

Form 5   Brush Knee and Twist Step (Left Style)

If the opponent forms a left bow step and attacks my left chest, abdomen or crotch with his right fist, I immediately draw in my chest and sink my body to lower my posture. After sitting firmly on my right leg, I quickly stretch out my left leg and raise my left hand, past my abdomen, to the place in front of my chest and gradually turn my palm obliquely outward to grasp the opponent's right fist or palm. Then, I take the opportunity to hold his wrist or forearm and neutralize his attack. In this way I can stay clear of the opponent's main force, and at the same time divert his force and draw his left force to my left side. At the same time, I move right hand forward to hit the opponent's chest with my palm. The movements of my legs and arms are synchronized with the turning of the waist. In this way I not only can make my actions well coordinated but can also move with speed and concentrated force, throw the opponent off balance and subdue him. (Fig. 24)

Fig. 24

Since "Brush Knee and Twist stop (Left Style)" sometimes follows "White Crane Spreads Its Wings" and sometimes follows "Hand Strums the Lute," or "Brush Knee and Twist Step (Right Style)" or "Turn and

Kick with Left Heel", the transition movements differ in each case, but the principle of application is basically the same.

Form 6　　Hand Strums the Lute

If the opponent hits my chest with his right palm or fist, I quickly turn my right hand from below the opponent's right wrist upward and hold it; at the same time I quickly raise my left hand to hold his right elbow. Then with the force of both hands I compel the opponent's elbow and arm to straighten. Thus, with my left hand closing in and pushing upward and my right hand pulling downward towards the right side, the opponent will be forced to lose control of himself. (Fig. 25)

Fig. 25

Form 7　　Deflect Downward, Parry and Punch

If the opponent attacks me with his right hand, I gradually clench my right fist and, with the waist leading, turn body from right to left to divert the force of his right hand to the left side by bending my wrist downward with the clenched fist; or turn my body from left to right to divert the force of his left hand to the right side by turning my wrist with clenched fist. This is called "Deflect Downward."

When I intercept the opponent's right hand with my left palm, it is called "Parry". When the opponent exposes his chest, I immediately hit it with my right fist. This is called "Punch".

The above explains how "Deflect Downward, Parry and Punch" is used. (Figs 26, 27, 28, 29)

Fig. 26

Fig. 27

Fig. 28

Fig. 29

Form 8   Apparent Close-Up

If the opponent holds my right fist with his left hand, I immediately raise my left hand from under my right elbow and hit his left wrist with the bend of my left hand. (Fig. 30)

If the opponent tries to use the other hand to push forward, I immediately open my right fist, draw it back towards my bosom, and then cross my hands obliquely to make the opponent unable to come forward. This is called "Seal". (Fig. 31)

| Fig. 30 | Fig. 31 |

I quickly place my right hand on the opponent's left elbow, turn my body, bend my left leg and push forward with both hands, which makes the opponent unable to escape or divert the force. This is called "Close-Up". (Figs. 32-33)

Form 9   Cross Hands

If the opponent attacks me from the right side, I immediately separate my arms to the right and left sides and then close them from below. Then, I turn my body along with the waist and legs, first to the right side and then to the left side. In opening and closing my arms, I exert my force on the inside of the opponent's wrists so as to divert his force and make him unable to come forward. When I turn my arms outward, my hands will be placed on the opponent's forearms. In this way, the opponent will lose control of himself and I push or hit him. (Figs. 34, 35, 36, 37)

Form 10   Carry the Tiger to the Mountain

Fig. 32

Fig. 33

Fig. 34

Fig. 35

If the opponent attacks me from the right side behind me, I quickly turn my body and separate both arms before knowing whether he is attacking with his hand or foot. While turning my right arm along with the waist to the right rear, I turn the arm and hand from inside outward and gradually change the hand from warding off to pulling back and then to pulling down, so that I can flexibly use my hand to counter the opponent according to the way he is going to attack me. But the main purpose is to force the opponent's waist to bend backward and incline his body so that

Fig. 36

Fig. 37

Fig. 38

Fig. 39

I can hit his shoulder with my palm. If the opponent attacks me with his fist from the front, I can take the opportunity to clasp his arm and wrist; if he attacks with his foot, I can also clasp his foot. Clasping the opponent by the waist accords with the name of this form.

If the opponent is not clasped by me because of his quick reaction but only falls back and then attacks me again, I immediately counter his

Fig. 40   Fig. 41

attack with "Pull Back", "Press Forward" and "Push". Therefore, this form includes "Pull Back", "Press Forward" and "Push". (Figs. 38, 39, 40, 41)

Fig. 42   Fig. 43

Form 11   Fist Under Elbow

If the opponent hits my back with his left fist from the left rear, I quickly move my four limbs along with the waist and turn my body from right to left. At the same time, I gradually change my left hand, with the palm facing obliquely outward, and move it horizontally close to the opponents wrist. Then, with the movement of my body I seize his wrist and, making use of his own force as he dashes forward, I pull his wrist forward, which throws the opponent off balance. At this time, I immediately draw his wrist inward and move it in a small arc in order to decrease his force, and move it from below upward and raise his left arm. When the opponent exposes the left part of his chest, I can hit it with my right fist. (Fig. 42)

Form 12   Step Back and Repulse
the Monkey

If the opponent grasps my left wrist firmly and holds my right elbow with his left hand, I am thus restrained by him and cannot move if I remain in my original position. At this time, it is necessary for me to step back in order to lure the opponent forward. I relax my waist and crotch as I sink a bit downward, turn my left palm upward, withdraw my arm towards the left rear and step back. At the same time, at that very moment when the opponent follows and presses in, I quickly turn my right palm to hit the left part of his chest. In this way, he will be caught unprepared and will be hit by me. Though in this form I am at first in a passive position, I can turn defeat into victory. This is because I use the method of retreat in order to advance.

There are the left style and the right style in this form, but the application, the body movement and the footwork are all the same. (Fig. 43)

Form 13   Slant Flying

If the opponent hits my head with his right fist from the right side, I immediately turn my body rightward, raise my right leg and take a step obliquely to the right side. Then, I take this opportunity to hold the opponent's right wrist with my left hand and hit hard at the opponent's right armpit with a big movement of my right arm. If the opponent again attacks me with his left fist, I can quickly bend my elbow to hit him or attack him with my back while he turns his body to the right. (Figs. 44-45)

Form 14   Needle at Sea Bottom

If the opponent holds my right wrist with his right hand, I immedia-

Fig. 44

Fig. 45

Fig. 46

Fig. 47

tely bend my right elbow and right leg, turn my body to the right and withdraw my right hand to the upper right side. (Figs. 46-47)

If the opponent takes this opportunity to attack me, I quickly bend my waist and sink downward and, along with this movement, move my right wrist away. (Fig. 48)

In this form, there are both the raising strength and the sinking strength. Though they are not used to attack directly, their sudden movement will catch the opponent unaware and I can seize the opportunity to attack him.

Fig. 48

Fig. 49

Fig. 50

Form 15   Fan Through the Back

If the opponent attacks me from below with his right hand, I immediately take the opportunity to turn my right arm and palm outward to seize his right wrist. Then I raise his right arm from below upward until it is beside my right forehead. At the same time, I raise my left hand to the place in front of my chest and hit straight at the opponent's ribs with my palm. (Figs. 49-50)

Form 16   Chop Opponent with Fist

If the opponent attacks my ribs with his fist from behind, I immediately turn my body from left to right, with my left foot turned inward, and change the left foot into an empty stance.   While turning my body, I gradually change my right hand into fist, and with the horizontal force of turning the waist and leg, hit or press the opponent's right wrist or face. If he dodges quickly and my right fist cannot hit him, I can turn my palm obliquely downward and take the opportunity to grip his wrist. At the same time, I hit at the opponent's face with my left palm. (Figs. 51-52)

Fig. 51

Fig. 52

Form 17   Wave Hands Like
Clouds on Both Sides

If the opponent attacks my chest or ribs with his right fist from the front or from one side, I quickly raise my left arm and gradually turn my palm from inside outward with the force of warding off slantingly upward. Then. as my left palm moves closer, I seize the opponent's forearm and wrist and, along with the turning of my body from right to left, divert the opponent's force to one side. In this way, the opponent comes under my control; and in particular his chest is exposed and I can hit it with my right palm. If the opponent hits me with his left fist, I use the same method to check him and hit his shoulder and ribs with my right palm.

What is described above involves turning the body to the left and using the left arm to divert the force of the opponent's right arm. If I counter the opponent's attack with my right arm, I should turn my body to the right. The crucial point in applying this form lies in turning my waist and crotch so as to upset his balance and shake his basis, thereby subduing him. (Figs. 53, 54, 55, 56)

Fig. 53

Fig. 54

Fig. 55

Fig. 56

Form 18   High Pat on Horse

If the opponent tries to seize my outstretched palm with his left

hand, I immediately turn my left hand from below the opponent's wrist upward, grip his left wrist and pull it down towards the left side of my body. Then, I shift my weight on to the right leg and draw my left foot backward. While the opponent is thus led in and inclines his body forward, I quickly bend my right arm and hit the opponent's face or neck horizontally with the outer edge of my right palm. If he attacks me with his right fist, I quickly push down his left arm with my right arm and raise his left wrist with my left arm and, with the force of closing both arm, keep him under my control. In this way, though his fist has come near me, it is powerless. (Fig. 57)

Fig. 57

Form 19   Separation of Right Foot

If the opponent tries to seize my outstretched right wrist with his left hand, I immediately turn my right palm outward and place it on his left elbow, while my left hand holds his left wrist and pull his left arm downward to the left side. At the same time, I stretch out my left leg to form a left bow step and raise my right leg to kick the opponent's left ribs with the instep straightened. I separate my arms to both sides to part his arms and hold his forearm and wrist. Thus, he is subdued by me.

"Separation of Left Foot" is the same as "Separation of Right Foot", only reversing "right" and "left". (Figs. 58, 59, 60, 61, 62)

Fig. 58

Fig. 59

Fig. 60

Fig. 61

Form 20　　Turn and Kick with Left Heel

If the opponent attacks me with his right or left fist from behind, I immediately turn my body from right to left and face straight to the front. Then I raise my left leg, with the toes pointing downward, and stand firmly on my right leg. Then, I quickly seize the opponent's right wrist with my left hand and kick at his abdomen with my left heel, with the toes pointing upward. When I turn my body, I first close both arms from outside inward, and when I kick with the left heel, I separate my palms at

| Fig. 62 | Fig. 63 |

the same time to the left and right sides. When I close both arms, I draw the pushing strength in; and when I separate them, I use my hands to pull, ward upward, push or bend backward. This is determined on the instant in the light of the opponent's stance. (Fig. 63)

Form 21   Step Up and Punch

Downward

If the opponent kicks my knee horizontally with his right foot. I quickly turn my body from right to left to ward off the opponent's right leg with my left hand. If that doesn't succeed, I quickly punch his leg with my right fist. (Fig. 64)

If the opponent hits my chest with his left fist and tries at the same time to kick me with his left leg, I immediately turn my body from right to left and turn my left arm along with the turning of my waist to seize the opponent s left wrist or ward it off. At the same time, I punch his knee with my right fist. (Fig. 65)

The movements should be well coordinated. At the moment of turning my body, I use the waist to lead the movement of the four limbs and strike out with my leg and arm all at once so as to catch my opponent unprepared.

Fig. 64 Fig. 65

Form 22 Hit the Tiger

If the opponent attacks me with his right fist from behind, I quickly turn my body from left to right and with the movement of the leg and arm seize hold of the opponent's right wrist and pull it downward. At the same time I change my left hand into fist and raise it to hit the opponent's head. At this time, I bend my right leg forward to give force to the blow. (Fig. 66)

Fig. 66 Fig. 67

If the opponent hits my head with his left fist, I also use the above-mentioned actions: turn my body from right to left, grasp the opponent's left wrist horizontally with my left hand and raise it, while my right hand is changed into fist to hit his left ribs. At the same time, I bend my left leg forward. (Fig. 67)

In Fig. 68 and Fig. 69, the applications and actions are the same as those in Fig. 66 and Fig. 67. The only differences are "right" and "left" "hit head" and "hit ribs", "pull arm downward" and "raise arm".

Fig. 68   Fig. 69

Fig. 70

Fig. 71

Form 23   Strike Opponent's Ears
with Both Fists

If the opponent attacks my head with both fists from the right side, I immediately turn my body and right foot to the right side and face the opponent. At the same time, I quickly move my two fists from above downward and use the back of the fists to separate the opponent's wrists and keep them pressed down. (Fig. 70). Then, I move my two fists from below upward and hit the opponent's ears with that part of the fist between the thumb and the index finger. At this time, following the movement of the waist, my right leg bends forward to form a right bow step while my arms ward off the attack by checking the opponent's movement of the elbows and make him unable to come forward. (Fig. 71)

Form 24　　Part the Wild Horse's Mane

If the opponent forms a right bow step and attacks me with his right fist from the right rear, I immediately turn my body to the right rear and glue my right hand to the opponent's right wrist. If the opponent exerts force, I immediately seize his right wrist with my left hand and at the same time stretch my right foot forward to form a right bow step and hit slantingly upward at the opponent's right armpit with my right forearm. (Fig. 72)

If the opponent attacks me with the same method from the same position, I can seize his wrist with my right hand. At the same time, I stretch my left leg forward and hit slantingly upward at the opponent's right armpit with my left forearm. (Fig. 73)

If the opponent attacks me with his left fist, I can use the above-

Fig. 72　　　　　　　　　　Fig. 73

mentioned method to counter him.

Form 25   Fair Lady Works at Shuttles

If the opponent hits me right on the head with his right fist from my right side when his right foot is in the front, I quickly turn my body left to the right. Then, I first hold the opponent's right wrist with my right hand and, with my right foot taking half a step horizontally to the right side, I sit firmly on it and raise my left hand, which is under the opponent's right elbow and place it between his elbow and wrist. At the same time, with my left foot taking a step forward, I sit firmly on it, change my right hand into palm and hit at the opponent's chest. (Fig. 74)

If the opponent, who is behind me on the rightside, also places his right foot in the front and hit me right on the head with his right fist, I quickly turn my body from the left slightly to the right and raise the opponent's right arm with my right forearm which remains glued to it. At the same time, I take a step forward with my right foot, bend the knee and hit at the opponent's right ribs with my left palm. (Fig. 75)

Fig. 74   Fig. 75

There are four movements in this form and they are respectively directions of four oblique angles. The first and second movements, o₁ style and the other right style, have been explained above. The third fourth movements, also one left style and the other right style, can be formed with the same method as the first two movements. (Figs. 76-7.

Fig. 76   Fig. 77

Form 26   Push Down

If the opponent holds my left hand with his right hand, I immediately lower my body and draw my left hand back to the front of my chest so as to lure him in and make him incline forward and lose his balance. (Fig. 78)

Fig. 78

If the opponent takes this opportunity to hit my left chest wih his fist, I can turn over my hand to hold his right wrist and pull it down towards my left side.

Fig. 79

Fig. 80

Form 27   Golden Cook Stands on One Leg

If the opponent withdraws halfway during the preceding form, I seize the opportunity to move my body forward and stand up along with him. At the same time, I lift his right wrist with my left hand and, following him closely, move my right hand forward and upward. (Figs. 79-80)

When my right hand comes into contact with the opponent's left wrist, I quickly seize it and pull it downward. At the same time, I raise my knee to hit the opponent's abdomen or kick his crotch with my foot. Thus, I can subdue the opponent either way (Figs. 81-82)

Fig. 81

Fig. 82

There are the Left Style and the Right Style in this form, but in both cases the usage is the same. (Fig. 83)

Fig. 83

Fig. 84

Form 28   White Snake Puts Out Its Tongue

The usages in this form are the same as those in Form 16. The only difference is that in Form 16 I use the fist, while in this form, I use the palm. Refer to Form 16 for the movements and essential points. (Fig. 84)

Fig. 85

Form 29 High Pat on Horse and
Go with Palm

If the opponent attacks my left side with his right fist, I immediately raise my right hand to the inside of his right fist and turn over my hand to grasp his wrist. Then, I draw in my chest and pull his right wrist down towards my bosom. At the same time, I hit straight at the opponent's face or throat with my left palm. Thus, the opponent loses control of himself. (Fig. 85)

From 30 Cross Legs

The usages in this form are the same as those in Form 20, only reversing "right" and "left". See Fig. 63 for reference. (Fig. 86)

Fig. 86

Form 31 Step Up and Punch
Opponent's Pubic Region

If the opponent attacks my chest with his right fist when his right foot is in the front, I quickly grasp his right wrist with my left hand, and as I turn my body to the left, I pull it leftward. Then I stretch my left foot forward and at the same time clench my right fist to hit the opponents abdomen or crotch. (Fig. 87)

Fig. 87

Form 32   Step Up to Form Seven Stars

If the opponent strikes downward from above with his right hand, I immediately stand up and move forward to the left. Then I change my hands into fists and cross them to form the shape of "Seven Stars" with the fists facing obliquely downward and ward off the opponent's right elbow from below. At the same time, I can also hit the opponent's chest directly with both fists. (Fig. 88)

Fig. 88

Form 33   Retreat to Ride the Tiger

If the opponent pushes me with both his hands when his right foot is in the front, I immediately withdraw my right foot, change my left foot into an empty stance and shift with weight on to the right leg. At the same time, I separate my two wrists, one moving upward and the other downward, grasp his left wrist with my right hand and ward it off upward, and grasp his right wrist with my left hand and pull it downward to the left. In this way, by throwing the opponent off his balance, I make him unable to come forward. Thus, I am in the posture of "riding the tiger". (Fig. 89)

Form 34   Turn Round and
Kick Horizontally

If I am attacked from the front and the rear at the same time and the situation is critical, I keep my right foot in the original place and quickly raise my left foot. Then I move it along with the turning of the body towards the right rear. First I use both hands and my left leg to sweep horizontally like the whirlwind at the upper and lower parts of the opponent and then pull his arm with both hands to the right and kick horizontally at his chest. (Fig. 90)

Fig. 89

Fig. 90

Form 35   Shoot the Tiger with Bow

If the opponent fails to hit me with both hands and tries to retreat, I immediately step forward, use my left hand to hold his right elbow and my right hand to hold his right wrist and heave his arm to the right side, thereby rocking him to the foundation. Then, while turning my body from right to left, I bend my right leg forward with the sinking strength, change my hands into fists and hit the opponent's head with my right fist and his chest with my left fist. (Figs. 91-92)

Fig. 91

Fig. 92

ABOUT THE AUTHOR

The Famous Teacher Yang Zhendou

The author, who is now 63, is the great-grandson of Yang Luchan (1799-1872), the founder of the Yang school of *taijiquan*, and the third son of Yang Chengfu, the finalizer of that school. He is now a member of the Coaches Committee of the Chinese *Wushu* Association and a member of the Wushu Association of Shanxi Province and vice-president of the provincial capital's *wushu* association. Starting to learn Chinese boxing from his father at six, he now has a history of over 50 years in exercising with *taijiquan*.

It is said that when the author's great grandfather was young, he had the luck to learn *taijiquan* from Chen Changxing, a well-known master of the Chen-school of *taijiquan* in Henan Province. Having mastered this art, he was recommended to be a teacher of Chinese boxing in an aristocratic